DJ Lynn

ROAD NOISE

LMP
Leaving Madmen Publishing

To Steve

Total miles driven: 12,200
States visited: 32

300+ national parks, aquariums, zoos, caves, national landmarks, art and history museums, theater, festivals, amusement parks, tours, and ghost towns, all the while horseback riding, camping, gem hunting, walking, hiking, canoeing, and beach-time

Highest temperature: 106 in Chicago (Chicago heat wave July 1995)

Felt even hotter: Jacksonville, Florida

Days of rain: 4

Lowest temp: 34°F in Yellowstone Park in July

Scariest drive: Bursum Road to Mogollon, New Mexico

Worst traffic: Route 1 Southern Maine
Road frustrations: (not counting cheap motel issues): 70+

Arguments (estimated): 15+

Times I annoyed him (estimated): 60+

Times I cried: 2 (privately, 5)

Times he was the voice of reason (estimated): 50+

Times we smiled and laughed: Most days

Road Noise Main Route
Not including minor stops, backroads and day trips

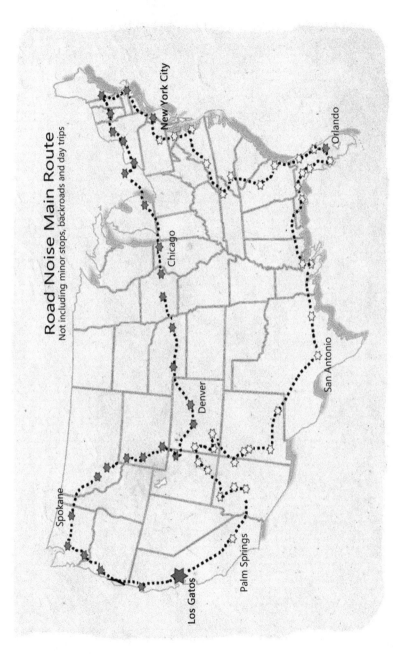

New York City

Orlando

Chicago

San Antonio

Denver

Spokane

Los Gatos

Palm Springs

Author's Note

We took the road trip in 1995 and although I had the technology of the day, much has changed since then. I had a new Toshiba 2150CDS laptop with a 520MB hard disk, 28MB RAM and an internal CD-ROM drive, a PCMCIA Megahertz cellular modem with FaxWorks, and a Motorola flip phone with Verizon Wireless. Although the Internet existed, it was in the early days before you could find every possible thing in the world. Google did not exist until late 1998.

My original journals and notes were on paper. When I got back, I input everything into Adobe PageMaker. Later I converted everything to Adobe InDesign and eventually into Microsoft Word.

School started in mid-August. I had an AOL email account. I worked with Steve's middle school months in advance to set up a *virtual classroom* so he wouldn't miss any schoolwork. The teacher and the principal were quick to accept the idea and work with us. Steve was in school on the road for nearly six weeks.

For maps I used CDs of *Rand McNally's Trip Maker* that I printed before I left. I also had the *Rand McNally Road Atlas* in the car. The general route is shown on the map, but I often took side roads, backroads, and coastal roads, avoiding Interstates when possible. Approximate miles covered was 12,200.

The vehicle was a 1994 Chevrolet Blazer

I used the real names of campgrounds, motels, hotels, hostels, restaurants, and other places we visited based on my notes and the ability to read my writing. In a few cases, I changed the names of places or people to protect their privacy.

The photographs in this book are my amateurish originals using a Nikon 35mm film camera with far more capabilities than I knew how to use.

For resources and links to places in the book, please check the author or publisher's website.

Contents

June 26, 1995-Leaving Los Gatos

A Corinthian wind bell stood silent over the wood deck of my apartment. It was one of the few financial splurges I had allowed myself particularly for items like a wind chime. The earthy moans of that thirty-six-inch chime had the rare effect of calming me when nothing else could. I carefully removed it, placing it in a box and into the back of my closet where it would stay until my return. Although I loved the rhythmic vibration, I thought my subtenant might not.

The anxiety beast that had been digging its claws into my shoulders for over a decade had released its grip. The little demon would likely be back. But for now, I felt my shoulders untangle and fall back into place.

After eight months of planning, the last details of the three-month road trip were falling into place. Constricted and judgmental family members criticized and didn't understand. What was my point?

Did I care if they didn't understand? Most people prefer certainty—as if there was such a thing as certainty—as if remaining in the same old patterns and places would assure a happy, contented future. I was used to it. I had long ago accepted them, but they never quite accepted me.

Was it me? Was I such an oddity because of my childhood growing up in an unconventional, oppressive religion? Was it the rape in high school by that obnoxious jock? Was it because my father died before I could get to really know him? My mother said I was a malcontent, never happy with the order of things, but that's what happens when your parents teach you nothing and shelter you from everything. *She was right; I wasn't happy with the order of many things.*

Maybe it was that turning point in my young life when JFK was assassinated. I still feel those moments when we all watched as the government lied to our faces. And it continued. It wasn't a one-off political *whoops* moment. As my years passed, I realized I was surrounded by a deeper pervasive pattern of lies I couldn't stop seeing or hearing.

To some people, I was a mystery, a curiosity—or maybe just one of those introverted philosophical types who kept to themselves, only venturing out to question the status quo and cause a stir.

That day, my son Steve and I were about to start an adventure, however tame it seemed—three months on the road, mother and son in a tightly packed new Chevrolet Blazer. The route was defined but not definite. Activities? To be determined. Reasons? So many. I was always on a mission. All my missions had plans and goals, but often something— usually someone—was stepping in front of me, shaking their head, wagging a finger, and demanding my conformity. This time, I would ignore them all. I wanted away from people—

particularly men (the grown-up ones, at least for a while) and time to think and create or just discover who I would be going forward.

. . .

It was another relentlessly sunny morning in Los Gatos, a small upscale town at the base of the eastern side of the Santa Cruz Mountains. Los Gatos was in the San Francisco Bay Area, a region known as Silicon Valley since a technology reporter started using the term in the 1950s. Almost everyone was in technology in some way. There was an attitude about that—a belief that there was something special about working and living there—about being one of those uniquely talented people that thought creatively—differently, as they would say. The offspring of the WWII grand mission had become pathological—big dreamers with massive egos. Narcissism and greed had become the caffeine that drove the dark side of the virus forward.

My son and I lived in a typical 1980s style two-bedroom apartment across the street from his middle school—one of the many deliberate moves I made over the years to keep him close to home since I was a single working mom. I instructed him to go straight home after school and call me. If he didn't call—he was in trouble. Trouble—such an arbitrary word. But that simple, meaningless threat worked for Steve. He never got into trouble except for his refusal to do most of his homework. It's not that he couldn't do it. He could remember much of what he read—at least the parts he thought interesting—and he was picky about what he thought was worth his time.

"Well, that is not the efficient way of doing things, Mom—not for me and not for the school system. We don't benefit from a system that pushes unnecessary information on us. It's a system of mediocrity for the masses. The world is different now."

I sighed again, one of many sighs in his proximity that echoed the impossibility of arguing with logic. *Where did he come up with that—mediocrity for the masses?*

Steve had always been wiser than his years. He had an unusual sensitivity to nature and an instinct for people he didn't get from me or his father. My friends called him an old soul—a young guru that saw into the heart of people. He was a thinker like me, never satisfied with surface observations. He sought details and explanations. He wanted answers and reasons, and as he got older, he recognized efficiency was the path to learning more, waving away the obvious parts of a problem and focusing on the center. When you dismantle the frills and excess, the cheap talk and exaggerations, the facades, and expensive suits, you find the base—the center of a problem and it is never what it looks like at the beginning.

Steve's old soul came with a weight attached. He was diagnosed with ADD when he was three years old. I was furious at the presumptuous pre-school teacher who pulled me aside after a long day of managing Steve's energy, however intelligent, clever, and entertaining as it was.

"Are you aware that your son has learning disabilities? He is displaying some traits that suggest he may not be suitable for this environment. You should have him tested."

Her tone was cool and condescending. She was young, inexperienced, and had no children of her own. What could I expect? She only wanted to manage kids that fit into the school's neat round holes—the ones she could mold into small replicas of herself and stamp out those who question too much of her authority—their authority.

What was she talking about? Steve was smart for his age—beyond his years. Yes, he had a lot of energy—better than some kid that sat around watching everyone else do things. It was her job to channel it—that's why I was paying extra for that overpriced Christian pre-school.

I didn't take the news well, but I took him to get tested. There were many tests—hearing, eyesight, blood tests, spatial reasoning, psychological questions, family history. It dragged on for weeks. The results were clear, but confusing. Yes, he was easily distracted, but he kept testing as highly intelligent. Back then, in the early 1980s, ADHD (some were just saying ADD—everyone seemed confused by the terms) was associated with a short attention span, hyperactivity, and lower IQ. But Steve wasn't hyperactive, had a high IQ, and had the ability to hyperfocus on things he thought worth his time.

Schools were equipped and structured to teach the masses and did not have the resources to deal with kids like Steve.

Many of his teachers wanted to send him to a school for the truly learning disabled. The only thing that kept Steve in the normal school system was my knowledge of the problem—both psychologically and legally—and the help of the school principals at every level. The principals at his elementary, middle, and high school levels supported me. The teachers—not all, but most—just wanted Steve out of their hair. I pleaded his case on a near-weekly basis, kept meticulous notes about every incident, call, test, and even what was in his lunch on the days his dad dropped him off. I made myself available to come and pick him up at the slightest provocation. Steve's father and I were divorced by then, and he was no help. He couldn't be bothered or even willing to believe his son had ADD. Instead, he regularly accused me of being too lenient with his discipline. I ignored many people's opinions and fought the rest, putting myself in their way from pre-school to high school. The system would not get around me.

But those challenges would come later and could fill another book. That day, as I was preparing for our road trip, what I knew most was how he loved to make me laugh and how he worried when I was sad. He was always trying to make me laugh by giving things funny names or using lines and voices from cartoon shows like *Shnookums and Meat, Earthworm Jim, Pinky and the Brain, The Simpsons,* and *The Tick.* He would often call me Meat or Pinky.

"What's on the schedule today, Meat?"

"Last bit of packing. Are you excited?"

"Yeah, I guess. I'm gonna miss my friends, though. Three months is a long time."

"Well, you'll come back a local celebrity. And your teacher is excited about her virtual student. Did you see the article about you in the paper? They're doing another when we get back. That's kind of cool, huh? And, we have a cell phone now so you can stay in contact."

I tousled his shaggy hair. Steve was nearly twelve years old, tall for his age, sturdy and coordinated. The only time I took him to the emergency room was when he pushed ham cubes up his nose when he was four. He said he did it to make some girls laugh.

. . .

Weeks before the trip, I measured the Blazer's rear space and marked it out on the living room floor with masking tape. I laid out all our supplies within the tape guidelines— arranging and rearranging for optimum use of space and efficiency, keeping everything as low as possible so I could see easily out the back window.

Camping supplies were in a separate trunk and positioned at the back hatch for easy in and easy out. Daily use things like the computer, Steve's books and games were kept near the front, behind my seat so he could reach back and get things he wanted without removing his seat belt. A week of food was kept in two ice chests—one had ice and kept the cold things and the other stocked munchies, cereal, rice, some canned goods, and other basics. I made sure there was always enough food to eat for a week if we had to—that is, if I got hopelessly lost driving some backroad, which I liked to do. Each chest was positioned at a side door, so they were easily accessible. In the middle of the car were several clear plastic totes and two overnight bags. The overnight bags contained a few clothes and toiletries. The totes—one for each of us, had additional clean clothes. There was also a separate laundry tote.

In the middle section of the car were books, supplies for school (when Steve started his *virtual classroom* portion of the trip in mid-August), and other things like computer supplies, software, coats, blankets, a tent, sleeping bags, and pillows. I also kept an emergency kit and supply of four gallons of water, a tarp, six flares, and a small toolbox.

And finally, attached to the back of the car were two bikes locked to each other and the car with two Kryptonite locks and chains. The whole thing was a work of art. The precision, balance, and use of space would have made an engineer proud. There was only one problem with the organizational precision; a pre-teen boy would be on board.

Details of the route were not planned. There were only hazy expectations of what I would see and feel and miss. Mostly, I wanted change and time away, even though I knew that in the end much would remain the same.

I wanted away from a job with a company that, for all practical purposes as employee number three, I helped start. I was patted on the back, given an office with a wide window and a door, a respectable title, and more responsibility. But in five years I hadn't been rewarded for that—no bonuses or raises and I knew others (the men) were getting them. Even when the company was merging and money was coming in, I wasn't protected or supported. I felt used. I traveled every eight weeks and got kudos from peers and customers and could say all the right things. I was knowledgeable, dedicated and a hard worker, but I was also a woman trying to ladder climb in Silicon Valley.

There is a mountain of responsibility that comes with being a mother, particularly a single mother—along with anger, frustration, and more guilt than most men ever experience. Not just guilt about something you've done wrong, but guilt that you haven't done enough—you haven't sacrificed enough—you haven't been flexible, understanding, or nice enough. You haven't thought of everything. That your entire life and that of your children is just one moment away from collapsing into a pile of rubble.

I wanted away from two divorces that battered and stole two decades of my life, wasted too much precious time, and tied an anchor of anger around my neck. I was slowly being choked of air.

I was responsible, too. I had nothing in common with those men; chosen for the wrong reasons. I was young, naïve, and impulsive. Can I blame my sheltered upbringing? Maybe. But at least I tried to grow. They didn't. Peter Pan, then a narcissist: unambitious, weak, critical, judgmental, manipulator. Still, the outcome was the same. Zero-sum game. I needed to release their mental hold on me; how else could I do it but to run? I needed time to think without the background rumblings of loud, monotonous men and whining women.

I wanted away from the memories of Jason, my third major relationship, and a man who had crushed my belief in the possibility of soulmates. He thought so, but maybe I never was a believer.

I wanted to escape my attempts to make sense of my odd childhood, jobs full of greedy narcissists, social and political distortions, and a restless mind as persistent as hovering gnats.

It began at noon that day. As soon as I shut my car door, simultaneously glancing over to see if Steve had buckled in, I could finally breathe. We were committed now—no going back, and I was determined it was not just about a three-month escape. I was not running away; I was running towards something. I just didn't know what.

Craving Sunlight

Redwood Hostel,
Redwood National Park

Small stones hit the underside of the car as my tires spun in the gravel driveway that rose to the entrance of the Redwood Hostel. It was 9:30 PM when we finally arrived. I wanted out of the car, but I wasn't sure I could move. Steve was already out and running up to the entrance.

Eight hours of driving was double the daily plan for this trip, and I felt twisted and pinched from the neck down. Outside it was cold and damp, typical for the Northern California coast. It had been a long drive from Los Gatos—nearly 400 miles.

I pulled a small flashlight from the console and moved in a circle around the car. I was looking for something—a mountain lion, the madman with the claw, bigfoot. It was just a mother's instinct. Check the grounds. Look for suspicious activity. Assess possibilities—cliff ledges to fall from, bodies of water to drown in, rocks to fall over, oncoming cars, vicious dogs, or perhaps alien craft looking for abductees. Take mental note. Keep most concerns to self. Motherhood rule number five—control obsessive worry over nothing. I frequently failed.

My forty-something aging eardrums fluttered in the nighttime silence. There was only the persistent rhythm of Pacific waves across the highway. I couldn't see them, only twinkly moonlit streaks tumbling onto the shore. With eyes blinded by darkness, my other senses woke up and I could feel the vibration of the ocean through my feet and smell the thick, briny mist. A black sand beach just over the road hugged the coastline crossing the border into Oregon, and I knew I would be up before dawn to sink my toes into the cold pebbles and shiver against the early gray fog.

"Mom. Oy—Mom! Is there a television in the room?" The silence was broken by Steve's sweet voice. It was still young, gentle, and childlike. His face was still smooth and round. How long did I have before his voice lowered and his legs got long and hairy? How long before he would reject my hugs?

"What? Oh, no. This is a hostel. Remember, I was telling you about what a hostel is? There might be one in the community room. You can stay up for a little while, but we're going to bed soon; we're leaving in the morning."

"Why aren't we staying here awhile? It looks cool. I want to go to the beach tomorrow."

"That water is cold, you know."

"I don't care. I don't mind the cold; I just like the waves."

"Okay, but just in the morning; we're heading north along the coast and there will be plenty more beach time. Besides, we've been to the Redwoods before. Remember our camping trip when we went tubing with your friend Mark?"

That pleasant weekend shot back into the front of my brain. A smile came to my face, recalling those two seven-year-old boys splashing and laughing all day in the shallow river. Those perfect moments get lost sometimes in the daily routines of undone homework and arguments over bedtime or Saturday shopping trips for new pants. For two days I sat on a lounge chair at the edge of the river with my favorite things—a book and a cooler full of snacks and iced tea. If every day could...

"Can I bring the boogie board?"

"Yes. But remember, we can only stay for the morning."

Managing expectations is challenging with an active child. I had to make a logical argument. *Because I said so*, didn't work. If I didn't have the right tone and presentation, talking with Steve could be exhausting.

Steve had already reached the entrance of the hostel. "Hey, hey, come back! Little help here." He ran back to the car with the same energy he had at 8 AM.

"Take this bag and that bottle of water." I pointed to my gallon bottle of distilled water I carried everywhere. He grabbed the bag and bottle and ran back up to the door like it was a relay race.

The hostel was an old two-story wood-frame house set just

off the road on a hill directly across Highway 101 from the ocean. A pony-tailed young man with a tie-dye scarf headband and a single black hoop earring eyed us strangely as we entered. I don't know why we got an odd look since I had called ahead, but I would realize later that the two of us would get strange or prolonged looks throughout the trip.

The clerk who made a point of telling me he was not the regular manager was abrupt, but not unfriendly, and for $28 offered us a private room and a list of rules. The rules included no shoes in the house, a closed kitchen after 9:30 PM (which it was), locked-in hours, and a request for us to be available at 8:30 AM to help with a chore. I glanced at the list—things like sweeping, watering the garden, and trash. I told him I planned to be up at dawn, in meditation on the beach, and out of there by 10 AM, but I would take the kitchen trash out to the bin before I left. He nodded in satisfaction and walked back to a wooden chair with frayed netting on the seat and picked up his book, *This Wheel's on Fire*. Immediately I heard lyrics of The Band in my head...

> *I said, "Hey, Carmen, come on let's go downtown,"*
> *She said, "I gotta go, but my friend can stick around,"*

Our private room overlooked a quiet deck and lush natural gardens. At least, that's what the cheaply photocopied black and white flier said. I pulled back the dusty curtain—a sheet hung on a metal rod. There could have been lush natural gardens, but it was too dark to tell, and I was too tired to find out. It could have been doobie weed for all I cared. Humboldt

County has always had a reputation for the private gardens that thrive among the public Redwoods.

A single chipped wooden chair with a lopsided leg stood in one corner and nearly toppled over as I threw my bag on the seat. On the other side of the room, a weathered and unraveling rattan table supported a plastic philodendron about to sprout a life form in its dust. Next to the fake plant was a stack of magazines. A quick flip through discovered both a 1976 *Field Guide to Pacific States Wildflowers* and a battered April 1972 edition of *Cosmopolitan*, the one with the Burt Reynolds three-page nude centerfold—a first in the history of male magazine nudes. There he was, still folded into the pages, arm strategically placed in front of him. A few former guests had penned comments or drawn pictures around the sides that resembled tongues or open lips and a penis or two. I got out my pen and added a drawing of kissing lips with my initials on them.

A metal clothing bar hung from the ceiling above the chair. Three bent wire hangers looked old and sad, but bravely clung to the bar. *How many clothes had hung on them, pulling them into this deformed shape? How many misfit relationships had hung on me?*

Although the accommodations were modest, the showers were hot; the bathrooms were clean enough and never occupied, and the two twin mattresses were semi-comfortable and bug-free—at least they looked like it.

As promised to ponytail man, I was up at dawn with the fog

and my Nikon all alone on the black sand beach while I let Steve sleep a little longer but left a note on the door and a pen on the floor in case he got up.

My lungs filled with the cool air from the ocean. I smoothed out a bamboo mat on the dark, pebbly California beach, pulled the hood up on my sweatshirt and sunk down cross-legged. I shivered against the cold as my legs hit the mat, closed my eyes, and listened to the waves to shut out the noise in my head. The sky was misty, but I imagined the sun on my face. I was craving some inner sunlight.

Meditation was a form of relaxation I started during the second divorce. It calmed my gut and kept the panic attacks to a manageable level. It may have been the only thing that kept me from losing my mind during those traumatic years. Time to feel whole again. I wasn't expecting a religious transformation—I just wanted a method to cope with my pain and panic and take myself to a place in my head that was calm and peaceful. I felt connected to something, but I didn't believe it was a personally attentive god. I was long past the god called on to answer the prayers of individuals begging for mercy, miracles, or money, or a personally desired outcome of a sports team. If there was a god of such glory as to put together such a multiverse—why would it waste time with individual specks of sand praying for personal gain? All anyone had to do was look around at the ugliness that had swallowed humanity. Prayers were either going unanswered or bad outcomes were excused away as god's mystery.

My belief in a connectedness was a philosophical one—a universal energy that connected us to everything. It swirled through these giant redwoods and every grain of sand on that black sand beach. Every breath in was a potential healing of body and mind. The force—the god—was within; every day was a choice to connect to that energy of the whole. We are just one sliver of bark in the Redwood Forest and one fast-dying spark in the biggest of forest fires.

Road Noise

Newport Views

South Beach, Newport, Oregon

A Barbara Bush doppelganger in hippie polyester leaned heavily on a scarred and scratched wood counter. I guessed she was over forty, but with more wrinkles around her mouth than usual. *Must be a smoker.* Upon seeing us, the sides of her dry, pale lips seemed to move at the corners as if trying to smile. On her hand was a plain wedding band so thin it was disappearing into her finger. She moved clumsily and slowly, as if she were high. A gritty man, who looked to be much older, appeared from the back. Two weeks of gray stubble framed his face and an unfiltered cigarette hung on his bottom lip when he nodded to us and uttered a gravelly welcome. He moved behind counterwoman, brushing against her as he reached around to stub out the soggy brown butt. His other hand dropped toward her backside and gave it a grab. She flinched and turned her head away from him; her fake smile flatlined.

I wondered how she ended up in this place. Did she choose it, or did she stumble, so accidentally, just to wake up one day and find herself behind this counter, married to this old man and selling dust collectors to pale tourists?

Road Noise

Who are the people that own roadside tourist attractions? Are they loners or tourist lovers? Pot growers or art patrons? Are they readers of *UFO Magazine* or *Atlantic Monthly*? Did they go to Harvard and opt-out? Did they have enough of urban madness and make an effort to buy a novelty gift shop gas station in the middle of nowhere? Are we all just one degree away from standing behind that counter?

These questions came to mind after the third stop at a pseudo-science gift-gas-dino emporium on a backroad to Coos Bay, Oregon. I had paid little attention to such places in my other travels, but this time I was coerced into stopping at many as Steve looked for his various treasures. He was particularly interested in miniature potentially pewter objects like dragons, dinosaurs, castles, and aliens.

He pushed a metal object toward my hand and was chattering about his new baby dino and handed it to me for purchase confirmation. The display said it was pewter, but I was doubtful.

"Nice choice, babe. He's cute, huh? Is he going to grow up to be a big terror *T. rex*, like you?"

He rolled his eyes at my joke-for-a-five-year-old as he dug in his pocket for money. "Whatever makes you happy, Mom."

I liked that look on his face—knowing me. He knew me well and often seemed older and wiser. He had more information than me, and I didn't know where he got it. I always felt old around him—like he had access to Akashic knowledge or another dimension. He learned without hesitation. *But all kids do; it's their innocent and uncluttered mind, but it was more than that with him.* He understood people but was never judgmental—everyone was an equal, as if we all grew up together and endured the same parental imbalance and failed milestones. Things didn't faze him as they did me. He was calm and rational while I was—well—not.

I was not so easy on people and preferred to be alone much of the time. On the occasions I had to force social interaction—it was timed and there was always an escape plan. Yet I was in marketing all my life—social interaction was my business. I managed it by controlling the details, at least until my anxiety forced a retreat.

Driving along coastal Oregon, we spotted several campsites directly on the beach and decided on South Beach near Newport. It was barely camping, more like pitching a tent in a city park. It had nice bathrooms, hot showers with doors and towel racks. There was running water and electricity at the sites. It was surrounded by tall pines and was nestled just over a ridge from the ocean that helped to block the wind but obstructed the view. Steve was disappointed because he wanted to sleep directly on the beach inches from the shore, but I imagined sand and crabs in my sleeping bag, hair, and underwear. I bribed him out of that option with a promise of smores, while pointing out all the benefits of being on the other side of the ridge. Even he didn't like the sound of crabs and sand fleas in his shorts.

It was 3 PM in the afternoon and 90 degrees. Sweat was trickling down my back. It would be our first-time making camp on the trip, and I felt compelled to set the pattern about how it should be done. Steve would comply because camping is all about the conservation of energy—efficiency, and he liked that.

I opened the back of the Blazer and unpacked selectively since we would be there only one night. I gave Steve specific instructions, as I had learned to do with him long ago.

"Take this tent to the clearing between those two trees. Lay it out the way I showed you when we practiced and face the door opening toward the campfire pit. Don't get it too close to the pit, though. I'm going to get the ice chests out and I'll be right there."

Simple enough. I carried the ice chests to the picnic table and went over to the tent. He had laid it out without bothering to remove the two large rocks in the clearing and now under the tent. But to be fair, I hadn't mentioned the removal of the rocks in my instructions. The tent opening was facing back, away from the fire pit, but he had smoothed the edges and had started to put the rods in the top. I removed the rocks and suggested we turn the tent toward the pit and then I let him hammer the stakes in the ground and abstained from telling him to be careful.

Once it cooled down by a few degrees, I asked if he wanted to build the fire. He scrambled up from his lawn chair, nearly knocking it over.

"Can I light the fire, too?"

"Sure, there are starter sticks and a lighter in the camp trunk, but you still need to collect some good wood—it needs to be really dry."

"Exxxcellent," he said in his Mr. Burns' voice, accompanied by the tapping of the tips of the fingers together.

He had voices and cartoon phrases to fit any situation. There were Krusty phrases, "Oy, what do I have to do to make you people happy?" On certain occasions it was The Tick, "Gravity is a harsh mistress." Or on any random occasion, Pinky and the Brain, "Pinky, you are a threat to tolerance." I looked forward to hearing them all and missed them when he wasn't in the mood.

He built a great fire, and we cooked chili and canned corn. Occasionally I boiled a bag of rice or cooked vegetables from a local farmers market. He liked the food, and I liked the cleanup. Afterward, we made smores, drank iced tea or milk and we always toasted something at sunset—the fall of a charred log on the fire, a noise coming from the next campsite, or the cricket that took an unfortunate path in front of me.

I had deliberately not brought along a portable television, and I didn't allow any Game Boy or computer games except while traveling in the car. I made a few exceptions on mornings when I just wanted to sleep in or have time to myself—but that didn't happen until later in the trip, when money and tempers were running short. Instead, we would play cards or trivia games by firelight or make up stories about some sound we heard. He liked to try to scare me, and he liked that I faked my fear—but I never tried to scare him in return. My fears were real; his were cartoon characters.

We usually went to bed not long after dark. I had a special tote bag outfitted just for the tent. There was a wooden tray that fit perfectly between the two air mattresses. It was big enough for a book, a battery-operated light, and the cell phone.

Steve was always asleep within minutes. It took longer for me—sometimes a lot longer. I listened to the sounds of South Beach well into the night. Some were just over the ridge— people walking and whispering on the beach; the sounds of lovers cuddled up on a blanket. I had thoughts of Jim, my young lover I last saw on my birthday just months before this trip and in a way, the catalyst for it—*the final straw*. Just two months later, in December 1994, he would die of leukemia at age thirty-two.

We met eight years earlier in Carmel on a back beach less traveled by the tourists. We would meet several afternoons a week, dig our toes into the sand, eat French bread and drink wine from Nielson's, and talk about extraordinary things. Our relationship then was platonic. We would never be an ordinary couple with our ten-year age gap and life paths that were going in opposite directions. It's easy then to talk about secret things and big dreams and support each other in ways no one else could.

Six months later, I would leave Jim and Carmel behind.

With divorce finally becoming reality, I moved back to Los Gatos thinking it would be easier to get a job. *A mistake now, I know. I wanted that divorce, but I shouldn't have moved. I would have been happier there; more content. I miss the ocean and the Cypress trees and foggy summer days.*

I didn't see Jim again for seven years. Then toward the end of 1993, he called, and for the next year we picked up where we left off except for two things; it was no longer platonic, and he was two years in remission from leukemia. We fell in love despite his quickening health storm and our age gap. It lasted almost a year. Once a month one of us would drive the ninety minutes between Monterey Bay and Los Gatos and spend the weekend soothing each other's souls and talking of nothing ordinary well into the night. Then a cold day in December arrived with his phone call; he had been admitted to the hospital.

He begged me not to come see him. "Don't worry about me," he said. "I'm surrounded by family and will pass gently. I want you to remember me as we were; and I want to leave this world remembering your smiling face."

A few tears rolled into my ears as I remembered those last words. Jim was gone and I realized the lovers on South Beach were gone, too. It was quiet now. I could hear the slow rolling waves and for just a moment it felt like I was on that Carmel beach so many years ago.

I woke up throwing the sleeping bag off. It was already hot. It was 9 AM and the temperature was climbing fast. I didn't know it then, but that summer would be a record-setting, heat-stroking, people-killing hot summer.

I leaned over Steve's air mattress, gave him a kiss on the head, tousled his hair and said, "Time to get up sweet pea. Let's go Frisbee on the beach."

Steve was never a sleepyhead and woke right away. "Will you build a sand robot with me?"

"Absolutely. First, I'm making breakfast. You want eggs and coffee?" I gave him a big smile, "Oh wait, you don't drink coffee!"

"Where are we going today, Meat?"

"North toward Seattle to see your friends Daniel and Eva. We're going to drive along the Oregon coast and stop at some more beaches along the way. Does that sound good?"

"Can I boogie board? Are you going to get in the water?"

"My toes will definitely get in the water, maybe even my ankles. But I don't think my knees are going to make it."

Carving Stories

Oregon Coast to
Kalama, Washington

The screen door of the cafe gas station novelty-shop bounced against a cracked wooden frame. A turn of my head discovered a young man in his early twenties walking tall and handsome into the room. He was there to tow away a junk car that must have been sitting quite a while since the skinny forty-something woman behind the counter seemed more than excited about his appearance. Limp bleached blond hair and toppling breasts flopped against her tight white tank that said, *Girls Kick Bass* as she jumped up, hands waving in the air.

"Johnny-boy, you're the man."

He winked at her as he slid onto a yellow pleather counter stool. "Anything for my best girl."

She blew him a kiss and set a plate of apple pie and a tall glass of milk in front of him. I stared at him over my cheese sandwich. He had the face and form of Jason, a man I once loved. Except for fewer pounds and years, he had the same blue eyes, shaggy fair hair, and high cheekbones. His height and body shape were the same. He even walked the same way with his shoulders pulled back and his chin up like he was either a GQ model or a gang member. He even wore his watch the same way—pulled forward in front of his wrist bone.

"I'm finally going to take that old car off your hands. I found a place that will take it for scrap."

"Thanks, Johnny. That thing haunts me, brings back bad memories, that accident and all. So, how is Jenny, did you guys make up?"

"No, it's over for sure this time. That woman is crazy. I need a more mature woman in my life." Then he turned his head toward me and winked.

Oh, great. I guess I'm the more "mature" woman. I smiled at him, but the sight of Jason's double reminded me of what I hated in him, not what I had loved—yet I still loved him— probably always would. I had kicked him out because he could not be his own hero. When he got lost in his past, he would hide in drugs and alcohol and that was a deal-breaker for me. I would not allow him to influence my son that way.

In the past few years, I had fully evolved into a lioness—a warrior and my son's protector. Last year, 1994, had been a winding down of men and madness—a purge of men who just wanted something from me but had nothing to give in return. Jim's death became a marker. I would choose more wisely going forward, or maybe there would be no permanent man in my life at all—at least until Steve was old enough and it wouldn't matter. I would think of men like dessert. I would try to avoid them except for the occasional short-term indulgence, usually resulting in remorse and quickly taking a digestive enzyme. But that was my mood at the beginning of this trip. In truth, I love men with passion and intelligence, if you can find them.

The men of the past were all gone now. Long since dispatched was Marley, the surfer-dude who spent his years during and after our brief relationship working as little as possible while waiting for his wealthy parents to die. With several inheritance payouts, he would waltz his way through several decades, barely working while spending every dime doing a lot of playing. Playtime included his wheeled toys like ATVs, dune buggies, and giant RVs to take his friends to Baja on surf trips.

Next, a rancorous five-year two-part divorce from Tom—who always thought he could fool me, twist words, and manipulate conversations with a variety of obvious lies and diversionary tactics. The result was that I tightened my rhetorical skills and refused to play his games.

After that, Jason, the hero who wasn't, and then Jim—sweet, handsome Jim, my young dead lover who reminded me that there were still good men out there. *Somewhere. Maybe. No, I'm sure of it.*

I looked at Steve and wondered if he noticed the man's similarities to Jason. He hadn't. He was intently examining the new candy he just bought.

"What are they?" I asked, not understanding what he just said.

"Too, T-O-O, Tarts," he spelled a little loudly. "I've never even seen these before! Try one."

"No, thanks." I scrunched up my nose. "I don't like sour candy."

Too Tarts were a liquid candy that came in a tiny bottle that should have cost about two cents. I found out later they cost him (actually, me) $1.25 per bottle. He would not find them again for the next 11,000 miles—and he looked. He searched every service station, gift shop, and corner market we came near for the rest of the trip for more Too Tarts, finally finding them again at a BP Station in Arizona. He saved them instead of eating them that time, carefully stashing them in his special tree-frog box we bought at the Florida Aquarium.

. . .

Kalama is a little town that overlooks the Columbia River and known for its fly-fishing—salmon, steelhead, catfish, and largemouth bass. But its true infamy comes from claiming the tallest single tree totem pole in the world and its sightings of bigfoot. Local lore claims about 500 sightings of the sasquatch throughout the string of forests that carve Washington state. Most sightings seem to come from rational people who swear it was not a bear or Uncle Eddie dressed in a fur suit. I wasn't a believer and Steve didn't seem to care, so we didn't go looking, but the artist and storyteller in both of us wanted to see the totem. The claim is that it is the largest one-piece totem in the world carved from a single 700-year-old Western Red Cedar.

My fascination with totems goes back to childhood and my father's love of Native American culture and found wood. He collected carved wood, petrified wood, twisted wood forms glued to black velvet-backed frames, and every sort of driftwood dust-collector found at local garage sales. They all sat in places of honor—on bookshelves that had no books—in our small old house at the edge of a new housing development near Denver they were calling Cherry Creek. He collected them because they were free, and we didn't have the money for store-bought tchotchkes, but they were also part of a grand source of nature he could hold on to. I would often see him holding a small piece of smooth wood, turning it over and over in his fingers while staring out our front window deep in thought.

Steve was sitting on the ground under a tree near the totem pole. He was looking up at the pole and then down to his lap; he was sketching something and showing it to the girl sitting next to him. She was older—maybe fifteen and seemed intently interested in his artwork. She kept throwing her head back in laughter.

I walked up and kneeled in front of them, "What's going on over here? What's so funny?"

"Mom, this is Jessie and I'm drawing her story with totem animals, well, more like Transformer creatures." He turned the book around to show me. "See, the bottom is a

Transformer bear that expands into a fox and then this weird looking guy that's sitting under a monkey and at the top, it's an owl with his wings stretched out and his claws in the top of the monkey's head."

Jessie looked up at me laughing again, "He's so funny."

"That's quite a story. Where did you come up with that?"

Steve explained, "Well, her family just saw bears in Yellowstone, and she has a stuffed owl, so…"

Jessie was laughing again and continued, "And then he added the monkey, and we decided the owl should carry the monkey, so he added the claws in the monkey's head."

I laughed. "Makes sense to me. Hey, you guys want to get pizza?"

The Long Collaboration

Seattle, Washington

Anna and her two rescued greyhounds greeted us at the door of her Seattle home she shared with her husband. It had been six years since I'd seen her or the kids. One of the last times I saw her was at her fourth of July party in Palo Alto with her former husband and friend of my former husband. We referred to it as the *fourth from hell.*

I was eager to catch up with Anna. Much had changed in the twelve years since we'd met in a small town outside of Boston on the Route 128 corridor. In Silicon Valley we called it the *other tech valley,* but it was really the beginning where the old giants behind the new giants originated, such as Raytheon, Bell Labs and Digital Equipment Corporation.

It didn't seem so long ago that we sat on her beautifully decorated porch swatting summer bugs, drinking lemonade, and sharing frustrations, mostly about our marriages and our static dreams. She was a beauty with flawless creamy skin and natural blonde hair. Back then, we were both midway through pregnancies just one month apart. While the pregnancy seemed to be just another day to her, I was barely walking, bent over like an old woman with pain in my back and legs. A few months later she gave birth to Eva and I to Steve.

Soon we all moved back to Silicon Valley as life was taking a hard turn into the chaotic. It was the early days of the Valley's super technology era. Life was moving so fast there was no time to focus on anything but kids and necessities. With both of our husbands working for the same technology company, we were all on the fast track. Companies were going public in months, venture capital was flowing, and egos were flourishing.

While our husbands worked long hours, traveled weekly, and suspicions of their infidelity grew, Anna and I spent more time together with the kids. We had lots to talk about. Kids were young. Marriages were crumbling and unhappiness all around fueled suspicions. Maybe it was the fast pace of our lives, but a storm was brewing. We both married hastily. We had our ideas of what marriage was supposed to be, but technology and the Internet were changing everything, creating a kind of insanity all around the Valley that everything was okay because we were advancing the future; that what we were building was so much more important than what we were destroying.

Anna and I had a mutual admiration for each other, but while I had big dreams and ideas, Anna was a woman with vision and focus. During a golf game in Pebble Beach, she told me she was intimidated by me.

I was surprised. "What? Why?"

"You're smart and have a technology career, your life is so put together, and Steve is so sweet and clever. And you always look good. Look at you, who wears makeup to play golf?"

"It's only mascara and lip gloss and besides, I need makeup and you don't. And my life isn't together. Our marriage is a mess. And, funny you say that because I'm in complete awe of you. You're so talented and creative and you know what you want. I only know what I don't want."

As we pushed chattering fair haired two-year-olds in matching strollers through the Stanford Shopping Center, we confessed our deepest thoughts about our marriages, past relationships, men, sex, and well, anything that came to mind.

With Tom's business relationship with the company ending, he decided we would move to Carmel. Anna and I were now living two hours apart and with jobs, growing kids, and traveling cheating husbands, it was hard to spend much time together. Still, we would meet once a month at her place to let the kids play together on a Saturday afternoon or meet without the kids for a couple of drinks and dinner in Carmel.

It was during those dinners we shared the details of our mutual secret; we had taken an interest in other men, and we were no longer going to just talk about divorce. A month later confessions were made all around, and a raging thunderstorm moved in and hung over our marriages.

Just a week later was the fourth of July and a party that had been organized for months. A substantial group of friends would gather to watch fireworks at their house on the hillside that had a sweeping view of Silicon Valley.

After all the party guests had gone home, the four of us sat around the living room, each in separate chairs. The body language alone foretold the conversation that had been festering from the beginning of the evening. We all knew it would not end well. Fueled with multiple bottles of wine and with allies on both sides, the conversation quickly turned into a shouting match full of accusations that reached back years, dredging up deep wounds and betrayals. Anna and I were also accused of having long collaborated and planned this cheating and divorce coup. For two hours the shouting, finger pointing and name calling continued until the men left the house for a local bar.

The men left. Not a surprise. Anna and I got up to check on the kids. Daniel, Eva, and Steve were sleeping peacefully all in one bed in the shape of a three-pointed star.

. . .

The greyhounds sniffed and nestled our hands. Anna and I hugged and kissed each other and the kids before the three of them ran off to the backyard to play.

"I'm so glad you stopped on your great adventure to see us. It's been a long time," said Anna.

"I've missed you. It was too easy to lose touch. My fault. Busy lives. That's been our story. But look at you; remarried and starting a new business. I'm happy for you."

Matthew, Anna's husband, came to the door with one hand out for a handshake, and the other holding a potholder.

"Great to meet you after all these years. Come on out back. I have drinks ready for you and I'm making dinner and taking care of the kids, so you two have all the time you need to catch up."

For the next day and a half, we caught up on stories old and new, walked downtown Seattle and the Pike Place Market, and let the kids linger in a card and game shop. It was the same thing we would have done ten years ago, except in those ten years she had turned her life around and zeroed in on her vision. She had become complete. I was still a shifting, drifting cloud. Formless. Shapeless. The difference between us then was still the difference between us now.

Road Noise

Useless Things

Spokane, Washington

Fifty miles east of Seattle, the landscape changed to thriving farmland. Local farmers posted signs that provided the interested with the names of the crops growing in the fields. Distant white swirls of a jet spread out in circles across the sky so far down the horizon that they seemed to close in on the rippled gray road.

Steve was on headphones and playing a computer game called *Doom*. I changed the CD to a compilation of Pink Floyd selections I'd made before the trip and pushed the pedal to seventy-five. It seemed too early in the trip for me to be feeling so melancholy; but for ninety miles on a straight, quiet backroad to Spokane, I silently reviewed my frustrations of recent years to the brooding mood of Pink Floyd.

I felt tired and confused. Did I miss something that everyone else gets? Why did I question things few people seemed to care about? People just believe what they are told, yet pieces of humanity were falling away. The lies were everywhere—for those willing to look. The dream is gone. It frustrated me that most people spent so much time in the

49

collection of useless things, and I don't mean assets and objects, I mean ideas and beliefs. Have we become so comfortably numb?

I never listened to much Pink Floyd until Jason. For him, it was solace for some childhood traumas he rarely spoke of unless we had too much tequila. Then he would pour himself out into a puddle on the floor, leaking all his secrets until he was sad and quiet again. I was his champion and his pillow, his priest, and his lover. We cried thousands of tears together, but four years into our relationship a time came when he could no longer envision anything good for himself. All that love and understanding, trust and sharing; in the end, it meant nothing. Love is no match for fragile egos and soon he dismantled himself piece by piece until there was nothing left for me to hold.

The music was a reminder of that ending with Jason and that this trip was a new intention—a final restoration of decades of giving in and handing over. I fought it until it would drive me to the edge where I had to decide to change or accept the failure and give up.

The year leading up to the trip had been the final act—a devolution, and the music of Pink Floyd was a dark star that demanded I see the truth in myself and in those I swore I knew. If we don't stare down the truth, then we build the walls, and our own myopic resignation will render us blind. There are no heroics in conformity, and most people are content with that. If you ask, *are you happy* their sad offer is, *well, I'm not unhappy.* I won't exist that way, not for long anyway, and yet I find those words slipping off my tongue—but only silently to myself.

What was my evolution? It was not that anticipated towel snap—a jolt of pain to flip me around in an instant. It took more than a decade to convince myself that all that acquiescence served no one. They were all just temporary acts of conformity. So much of that stood and was tolerated. *No more,* I thought, but how would this three-month journey facilitate a new beginning? This road trip might just be a lot of driving, eating at mediocre cafes and buying T-shirts and city-named key chains. Was I just biding time? Was I running from the past only to re-live it again in the future? The road of transition is a steep, winding rocky path that, regardless of how hard the climb is, might still lead back to the beginning.

Aren't we all caught in a cycle? We are not unique like we once believed. The child is grown, and those dreams are gone and there I was—middle-aged single mom with few options and driving a dusty backroad to nowhere.

With your nerves in tatters, you better run.

. . .

The Spokane Hostel was a two-story old Craftsman-style house in a kindly kept residential section in the south part of the city. Tall pines stood over the street, providing an insufficient cover from the staggering heat—over 100 degrees. Manicured yards and neatly lined-up cars on the street guarded framed porches with summer wreaths and rocking chairs, wind chimes, star-shaped sun catchers, and cats licking themselves on cracked concrete steps. The house was a beauty at one time but had sagged under the burden of a few decades. Still, a dim charm remained, but you had to squint for it.

As usual, we got a confused look from the desk manager. *Woman and child traveling alone? How curious. Was it?*

The carpet in each room was different, salvaged by do-gooders for function, not continuity. In our room, it was a dingy yellow-gold shag that had become rough and stiff since the 1970s. The black and rose tapestry pattern of the entry hall carpet looked to be original. It may have come from my Aunt Ruth and Uncle Elmer's 1920s Pittsburgh sitting room along with the paintings and lamps. A little mahogany stained footstool with tapestry fabric and maroon fringe stood alone near a dark velvet green sofa.

Hum. Tiny footstools—a decor curiosity. What purpose does a tiny footstool serve? It's too small and low for a footrest and too fragile and short to be used to put away a book on a tall shelf. It's a decorative tripping hazard, and it reminded me of the small slip-and-die rugs my mother used to put in odd places around the house. Believing they were decor failures besides slipping hazards (my mother had little decorative sense), I would move them. The next day I would find them moved back to their previous location until one day she confronted me.

"Why do you move the rugs?"

"Because you put them in weird places. I'm surprised dad hasn't slipped on one. I've almost slipped on one myself. They have no grippy stuff on the bottom and they serve no purpose, so why have them?"

"Because they add color to the room, and we can't afford big rugs."

Oh god. Poverty logic. "Well, I just don't like them. Can't we add color some other way? I'll paint an accent wall."

"We can't afford paint, and besides, it's my house," she said in her definitive tone while walking away.

The slip-and-die rug debate with my mother may have summed up the whole of our complicated relationship; we had fundamental differences and strong personalities, yet I had absolute respect for her courage and strength of character.

A sweet, familiar voice interrupted my random thoughts about tiny footstools and slip-and-die rugs as he claimed one of the twin beds by tossing his overnight bag on it.

"This place is cool. I'm going outside to check things out. Wanna take a walk to that park we saw?"

I nodded. "Yes, but we're jogging, I need some exercise. I'll change and meet you out front in fifteen."

In the kitchen, as I packed a couple of sandwiches, I met two men who looked to be in their late 30s.

"I'm David and this is my business partner Kenny. I assume that was your son we just met. A very personable young man."

David produced a broad smile that revealed deep dimples on a tan, clean-shaven face. He was strikingly handsome with dark eyes, long fingers, and a neat white shirt tucked into light tan pants.

Did he say partner or business partner? I couldn't quite remember, but I noticed there was no ring on his finger. What was I thinking? We were two winds going in opposite directions and there would be no collision of warm fronts in Spokane tonight.

I smiled. "That's Steve. He's a character. He's looking for lizards. He's a nature guy—lizards, insects, frogs… I'm not supposed to step on ants."

"Yes, a character," David laughed. "He introduced himself, shook hands with us and asked us to wait up. Said he wanted to chat with us later. I wish I could say we could, but we're going out. I have a feeling I would enjoy a chat with Steve. Maybe we'll get a chance tomorrow."

Kenny laughed, "He'll find a lizard or two. That's basalt rock. Lizards love it. There's a lot of that in eastern Washington."

"Kenny knows. He's a naturalist and I'm a photographer and we're putting together a Washington State field guide. We're nature guys too. So, what are you two doing here?"

I told them the short version of the story I would tell a hundred more times during the next three months. Everyone was curious about the mother and son traveling around the USA. Most just asked where we were going and what we had seen. Few asked why, but I liked it when they did. Still, I didn't offer many insights into my convoluted life story.

Outside, Steve was pushing a stick into a crack in the wall. "There's an alligator lizard in there. I almost caught him."

"That's great. You know we're not bringing any along with us, right?"

Steve looked up and grinned. "What if I put him on a leash and fed him my cheese sandwiches?"

I didn't answer, but threw him the backpack, "Catch. You're carrying this."

We jogged to the park and ate sandwiches sitting on the root of a massive white willow tree. Later that night, in a city I had never been to before, on a bed that was not my own, I glanced around the sparse old room with mismatched furniture and smiled and I noticed I wasn't just *not unhappy*. My mood of earlier in the day had lifted. I felt happy, calm, and even peaceful. And according to my inquiry to Steve, he was too.

From the twin bed next to mine, he looked up from his book. "What? Happy? Yeah, sure Mom."

Road Noise

Rain on the Geysers

Butte, Montana to
Yellowstone Park

A small brown sign off the highway simply said *Fishing Access*. The markers appeared every few miles and were indistinguishable from each other. If you want to fish in Montana, you better know where to go. I passed quite a few simple brown signs before I realized I needed to just pick one. This was angling for real men—guys with plaid shirts, waders, and glow balls. Although I am hardly a girly-girl, I felt out of place. Steve even seemed to be embarrassed to be seen going fishing with mom. He knows that I have never been a typical female, but, on some occasions, I've reminded him. Where's the rule book that says because I'm female I was born to cook and pick up his socks? I hate the laundry, I never iron, and my cooking is more campfire than cuisine. Instead, I could converse intelligently about graphic cards and megabytes of RAM, figure out a cool science project, and kill spiders without screaming. I had white water rafted, hiked, skied hard, played a decent game of golf, and I don't mind getting dirty if there is some sort of showering device nearby. Most times those abilities didn't matter to him or had gone unnoticed.

I pulled off the road at the next Fishing Access sign and drove a mile down a gravel one-lane road. I stopped the car at a red steel bridge and noticed a small sign that designated it the Atwell Bridge. It would be one of the many strange coincidences I would have on this trip. Part of this journey was to escape my traumatic break up with Jason and now his last name appeared on a sign down a randomly chosen backroad near Big Sky, Montana. It was the second time in four days his name or body double had materialized.

I heard Steve dislocating the fishing gear from the back of the Blazer. I hurried to the back to avoid permanent damage to my sweet organizational setup. Steve was excited. I was excited. We were going to fish—where real men fished.

The Gallatin River at this location looked more like a rocky stream. It seemed shallow enough to wade to the other side, but a hefty current would make that dangerous. Smooth flat rocks lined the riverbank and swirling white fluff from the cottonwood trees hung in the air. Steve hooked on a lure I let him pick out at a local shop. It was a silvery rubber fish-object. It seemed too big for the size of this stream, but what I knew about fishing could fit inside a tackle box with room left over for a big lunch, so I didn't say anything.

Steve hurried in front of me and seemed to want to be alone or, at least, not be seen with me, so I found a wide rock, sat back, and turned my face to the sun.

Snowy cotton puffs tumbled onto my cheek. Meadowlarks

drowned out the sound of my deep breaths and other than rolling water over stones, it was quiet. There was no sound from the highway, no cars on the gravel road. No kids tubing on the river. There were no leaf blowers, no airplanes overhead, and no thumping boom-box at the intersection, no graffiti on the bridge, and no one standing right up behind me at the grocery checkout so close I could smell their onion breath. Nothing but the meadowlark and the short, muffled dialog between the only other two people at the river—two fishermen standing about forty yards upriver. I wondered if the men felt the same tranquility as I did. Did they feel the sun on their skin and notice the meadowlark? Did the cotton swirls soothe them or were they just an annoyance they brushed away when the puffs tickled their noses? Did they feel anything at all, or were they just fishing?

I watched Steve move toward them—close enough to speak. I couldn't hear the conversation, but I could see the quick response they gave him. They did not want the company of a young, male-companion-starved boy. They hustled him away and I felt a flurry of anger at them. A few minutes later they moved further upstream. I realized then that they were just fishing. I could sense Steve's disappointment but did not bring it up.

I moved to a rock close to him and tried to make general conversation about fishing and asked him how he knew so much about it. There was little response as he had turned his focus to hooking another lure. If the exchange with the men had bothered him, he didn't let on.

The afternoon wore on, but he caught no fish. He blamed his fishing inability, and I blamed the time of day, and we set off to find a place to stay the night before heading to Yellowstone. It turned out to be the Skookum Motel in Butte. I found out years later the lounge was a gay hangout. Had I known then, I might have stopped in and slammed down a Jack Daniel's with the real men of Montana.

. . .

It was only a couple of hours south of Big Sky into Yellowstone National Park, a place that held strong memories of my father. Thoughts of him filled my head like confetti and fluttered around in tiny colorful pieces; that's how I knew him, in disconnected fragments. Winfield was a colorful, gentle, trusting optimist, a leader in his church, and a man of his word. He was a man that thought for himself—and in the kindliest of ways didn't care what other people thought. He was a picture of a man as humble as Gandhi and as charismatic as Tony Robbins.

He liked to match his shirt with his socks. Although difficult to find a men's matching combo of that sort, he had a favorite short sleeve gold pinstripe shirt and gold socks. He wore his colored socks with his Knapp shoes and bragged often that he had only bought four pairs as an adult; each pair replaced by a new pair as they moved down the rank to back-up Knapps, to around-the-house Knapps, to lawn-mowing Knapps. They eventually made their way to a thrift store, completely battered and scuffed. He refused to throw them out, believing there was always someone worse off than him that could still make good use of them.

He had a weakness for cream pies and Pepsi and several heart attacks and diabetes complications later, his sixty-one-year-old heart gave up. But long before all that, I remember the three summers the family spent camping in Yellowstone.

My brother and I were young—single digits, but I remember bears in the road and clanging trash cans in the middle of the night. I remember wading in creeks so cold my feet were numb, climbing on rocks I thought were mountains, and worrying about falling into hot bubbling geysers that would suck me under into middle-earth. We listened to my father describe every geyser and rock formation like an expert. He was in awe of every type of wildlife but had a special love for the grizzly bear. He believed that one day soon when the earth was renewed by god, he could sit with one and stroke its fur to calm it during a storm. He believed it so completely that any thought of this salvation calmed and comforted him. He and my mother were missionaries before I was born, and they believed absolutely that the end of the wicked world was near. I grew up believing each day might be the last of the world I knew.

It took longer than expected to wind our way to the campsite in Yellowstone. It was drizzling, and the traffic was heavy and slow as everyone stopped to photograph an elk or a bear at every turn. It would be dark soon and the misty drizzle would soon turn to rain. The temperature had dropped to 54 degrees, and it was getting colder.

We found our campsite and I hurried Steve. We had just finished pitching the tent when it started to rain. I quickly grabbed the sleeping bags, overnight bags, and pillows from the car and threw them into the tent. We would eat dinner at the lodge, hang out at the gift shop for a while and then come back to camp and just jump in the tent for bed.

The Old Faithful Lodge was busy, loud, and full of people escaping the rain for the evening. The temperature had dropped to 38 degrees and the prediction was for more rain over the next few days. The expectation of experiencing Yellowstone with Steve the way I had when I was a kid was drowning. We prolonged dinner and shopping until 10 PM, then returned to the campsite. We burst out of the car and ran through the pouring rain toward the tent. I opened the zipper only to find the tent with two inches of water. In my haste to get out of the rain, I hadn't pulled the zipper all the way down and over the bottom flap. The sleeping bags, pillows, and the few other things I had thrown in were now wet.

I stood there in shock with rain pouring down my nose. While I uselessly ranted and raved at the weather and bad luck, we became wetter and wetter.

Steve was grabbing my coat sleeve, "Mom, we can't just stand here. I'll get the tarp from the car and we'll wrap everything we can from the tent in that for now. There's still some dry stuff in there; we'll put it in the car and figure it out in the morning."

Now sobbing, I said, "Yeah. Okay. Get the tarp. Oh god, the car will get muddy and wet inside."

Steve came back from the car holding the tarp open the best he could while I grabbed everything from inside the tent. We balled it up and threw the whole mess of wet plastic in on top of everything else in the back of the car. Leaving the tent standing, we drove back to the lodge to find a room. The thought of how much a room at the lodge would cost during high season was making me panic.

The woman at the counter seemed only mildly concerned about our situation but made a phone call to the park lodging center, then calmly apologized that the entire park was full. It was peak season, she reminded us. We went back out to the car, and I sat and cried. Steve was calm and desperately tried to comfort me. We had no choice; we would sleep in the freezing car. But the car was packed tightly and there would be no way we could lay the seats back or unpack the car. And then there was the cold. It was now 34 degrees and our clothes, sleeping bags, and pillows were wet.

"I can't believe this is happening. We have no place to sleep."

"It's okay, Mom. We can sleep in the car."

"We're going to be too cold," I sobbed.

"We'll be okay. It will be okay, Mom. I promise."

My young son had become the adult and I, the hysterical child. I remembered the rainbow he colored for me when he was four years old, and I was crying about the mess of my life and pending divorce. He pushed it into my hand and said, "Here mommy, this is for your tear-twinkle." And there he was, so many years later, still trying to fix my tear twinkles.

I looked at his face, wet and worried. He didn't care about the cold or the rain, or the mud trickling into my seats; he was worried about what I would do next.

I mentally gave myself several hard slaps to the face. *It's just rain! We're in a parking lot with a billion other cars, not the middle of the Yellowstone wilderness.*

I reached over and smoothed his wet hair, "You're right. Of course, we'll be fine. I'm being silly. Let's find some dry clothes and see what we have to cover-up with."

"Mom, this blanket is still dry and so are the towels."

We put on dry pants, several pairs of socks, our damp-on-the-outside jackets, covered ourselves with the blanket and towels, and the inside of a sleeping bag that was only partially wet and tried to sleep—upright in the seats.

Every few minutes I woke up trying to re-form my body into some other uncomfortable position around the steering wheel. Every hour I would turn on the engine and heater for a few minutes to keep Steve warm. He was not a small boy but somehow, he was curled up in the passenger seat with his head on a couple of towels and every time I looked, he seemed to be sleeping peacefully. I stroked his hair and pulled the blanket up to his chin.

Shootout in Jackson

Jackson, Wyoming

A steel blue sky was morphing into the day's wet gray haze. It was dawn in the parking lot of the Old Faithful Lodge in Yellowstone National Park. I woke doubtful I had slept at all. My feet were freezing, and I felt like someone had snuck into the car in the night and beat me up. Every bone hurt and my head was pounding. The rain had turned to drizzle, but that looked like a temporary reprieve. Away from the parking lot, it was a mudhole. I assumed the tent was still at the campsite— or maybe it had floated away. *Why hadn't I planned better for the likelihood of rain on this trip?*

In those waking moments, while Steve still slept in apparent comfort, curled up in the passenger seat, I contemplated a plan. What would be the fastest and most efficient way to take down the tent, roll it up and stash it in the car with the least amount of water and mud accompanying it? It would take teamwork. I woke Steve to go over the plan so we could execute it in the shortest amount of time. Even as a kid, Steve appreciated the benefits of efficiency.

Steve, probably believing I was still just a quirk away from a re-enactment of the previous night's breakdown, listened carefully, and executed the plan beautifully. The plan involved simultaneous un-bundling of the tarp and its already wet contents from the back of the car and spreading it on the least muddy section of the campsite. I would then remove the rods while Steve collapsed the tent. Then, we each took a side of the tent and tossed it on the tarp, folding it all into a new and flatter shape and then cramming it back into the car. It was one big bundle of soggy, muddy plastic—dripping onto all the other stuff in the car. Although, planning had paid off; most items were in plastic bins. But my seats? I could almost hear the mud worming its way into my beige fabric folded-down seats.

Since the rain was not letting up, we decided Yellowstone was not meant to be on this trip. Twenty minutes later we were outside Yellowstone and heading south past the Grand Tetons following the Snake River along Highway 191.

All I could think about was coffee when a drive-thru espresso place appeared. A gigantic latte and several cookies never tasted so good. In moments, the caffeine swirled in my blood, jolting back the memory of last night's tantrum over a minor travel setback. We were caught in the rain, things got wet, we had to sleep in the car sitting up and we didn't get to see much of Yellowstone. I overreacted, I cried, I was irrational and out of control. Anxiety and panic strike again. *Sigh. Mothering abilities in question—yet again.*

"How's your hot chocolate? And sorry about last night. I overreacted. I don't know why I wasn't prepared for rain."

"Mom, it's cool. No big deal, we'll see Yellowstone another time. And this hot chocolate is the best I've ever had."

. . .

The days were already running together. I had to rely on Steve's watch to provide the date and day of the week. It was the second of July and lunchtime as we pulled into Jackson. The Antler Inn was downtown and a block away from a laundry facility, at least nineteen lounges, twenty-six restaurants, and about 497 gift shops. Perfect.

Although the surrounding country is majestic, the town of Jackson is a movie set. It's artificial and overpriced—one big dude ranch.

We lunched at the Sportsman Cafe and wandered the town. Steve wanted to cross the street to talk to two men on horses in cowboy costumes, or maybe that was just their normal way of dressing. I popped into an expensive-looking gift shop and bought a $45 pendant with a bear underneath the moon and stars.

Outside the shop, I saw Steve across the street with the two cowboys. Steve was pointing at me and then they all waved. He crossed the street breathless and excited.

"Hey Mom. Did you see those cowboy guys? They're in a parade tomorrow, then there's going to be a fake gunfight in the town square at noon. They said they would pretend to shoot me if I stand by the steps at the antler arch. They said I have to fall down dramatically and pretend I'm dead but then get up in a few seconds and wave, so people don't think I'm really dead. Can we go?"

"Wow. That sounds amazing. And yeah, I want to see that. Do you have a plan for the dramatic fall?"

"Yeah. First, I'm going to fall back on my butt and then kick my feet up in the air and fall backward on my back. How's that?"

"Sounds perfect and very dramatic. Will you help me do laundry first in the morning? We need to clean up the tent mess in the back of the car."

"Sure. I'll help you, Mom."

The next day we were up early, did the laundry, cleaned the tarp and tent, and cleaned and repacked the car, then went to see the parade. Steve stood across the street from me in the designated shooting place. I worried they might disappoint him.

I wiggled my way to the front of the parade spectators and sat cross-legged on the ground. To the left sat a family group, mom, dad, and three kids that looked to be all under the age of ten. To the right sat a man, perhaps in his early forties, with a large hiker's backpack in front of him. We glanced at each other and smiled. He had a stubble beard, pale blue eyes, and dark wavy hair. His skin was fair but tanned, and the wrinkles around his eyes and mouth only enhanced his rugged good looks. He had on quick-dry shorts and well-worn hiking boots.

Oh, how I love a buffed-up adventurer.

Emboldened by the Yellowstone meltdown and determined to assure myself I still had some sort of tenacity, I decided to talk to the guy.

"That backpack must weigh as much as me, where are you hiking?" I held out my hand, "And hello, my name is Debbi."

He pushed his hand into mine, "Hi, I'm Jackson."

"Wait, seriously, you're Jackson and we're in Jackson, or are you giving me a fake name so I'll go away? That's okay if you are, I understand."

"That's my real name and please, don't go away. I'm just here for the night and thought I'd check out the gunfight. Meeting a friend at the Granite Canyon trailhead tomorrow. That's in the Tetons. Know anything about backpacking?"

"Absolutely nothing, but I'd like to know. With that size of pack, I assume it's more than a day hike. Where are you going?"

He laughed, "Definitely more than a day hike. If you really want to know, I'll give you the details, but in case I get lost, you have to promise to come and get me."

I laughed, "Then we'd both be lost, but I promise to send big helicopters and a massive search party."

"Deal. Well, we start off at Marion Lake and then continue along the Teton Crest Trail on Fox Creek Pass to Death

Canyon Shelf. The plan is to reach Hurricane Pass and see Schoolroom Glacier. Then we continue north past Avalanche Divide to South Fork Cascade Canyon. Eventually, we'll reach Lake Solitude. If the weather holds, we'll go straight up to Paintbrush Divide, elevation about 10,700 feet. Then we work our way down and exit at the Leigh Lake trailhead. About forty miles if we don't get lost or killed by a bear, but don't worry, we brought some bear repellent and we try to camp upwind."

"Those are all real names, right? Because they sound like cartoon places."

He laughed. "What about you? You seem to be a single lady, why are you here?"

"Single, yes, but not here alone. I'm traveling across the country for three months with my son. He's almost twelve. He's supposed to be in the show today. He met some cowboys yesterday that promised to shoot him in the show."

"Oh, I want to see that. Where is he?"

"He's standing over there under the antler arch. Blue shirt."

Jackson gave me a big smile, "If you don't have any plans, do you and your son want to have dinner with me later?"

The cowboys did not disappoint—they pretended to be afraid of Steve and then pulled out their guns and shot him. Steve added even more drama to his fall by clutching his chest and wavering around before falling on his butt with feet in the air. Three seconds later he got up and when the crowd clapped and cheered, he took a bow. It was quite a day.

Dinner was celebration pizza at a cafe sports bar with Jackson the backpacker. Rock music was playing from a speaker and an assortment of tourists in denim shorts, flowered tops, and baseball caps laughed loud and tossed down beer and jalapeno poppers.

I held out the last piece of pizza to Steve, "I'm proud of your acting today. That was quite a performance. How did you get those guys to do that?"

"I was just talking to them about the horses and then they asked me if I was on vacation, and I told him about our trip. They thought it was cool. I told them about Yellowstone and how we didn't get to see it cuz of the rain. I told 'em you kind of had a meltdown."

"You told them that? Oh, no. I'm totally embarrassed now."

"Why? They just thought it was funny."

"Yeah," I sighed. "I guess maybe it was kind of funny."

"Hold on," said Jackson. "Your mom had a meltdown in Yellowstone?"

Road Noise

Fire at the Hole

Green River, Wyoming to
Red Canyon, Utah

All four tires kicked into gear and maneuvered the unmarked rocky path up a hillside in Green River, Wyoming. For a while, I followed an old red pickup truck with a back full of coolers, chairs, boxes of fireworks, and two teenage boys with beers already in hand. Feeling braver, I moved to his left and climbed higher to take a rougher part of the road toward the cliff tops before coming to a stop near an old graveyard. High on the ridge, I could see the grassy valley below that swept into northern Utah. The sky was blue ear to ear and the sun so orange Steve said it looked like a tomato squashing down on the horizon.

If there were rules about off-roading up to the cliff tops, no one was paying any attention. There were no paved areas—it was just the flat and rocky top of a cliff. You could drive right over the edge if you wanted. No rails. No rules.

There were at least twenty cars loaded with people setting up their barbecues and fireworks. The smell of grilled meat was already in the air along with the buzz of Independence Day fireworks and beer-fueled partygoers.

I suddenly felt ill-prepared for a party of this magnitude. All I brought was a picnic dinner of fried chicken and cob corn from a local market and some pathetic fireworks. Too late now to remedy that. I set up our lawn chairs and Steve set up the fireworks. We ate fried chicken, people watched and played cards until 9 PM.

Green River sits at the mouth of Flaming Gorge and Firehole Canyon, which sounds like fireworks ought to be going off all day, every day. It was the perfect place to spend the fourth of July. It didn't take long to go through the fireworks I bought, which were the wimpy ones, anyway. I saw Steve watching a large family group full of kids who were setting up some big fireworks. I told Steve to go ask if he could watch. He did, and they seemed happy to have him join them. I stayed by the car and watched. *Why didn't I go over to the group with him? Why did I think I didn't fit in?*

It was nearly midnight when we got back to the motel. On the inside, the motel was like other cheap motels—no-frills, musty smell, seemingly clean sheets, and a bad air conditioner. The Flaming Gorge Motel had peeling paint and a gravel parking area. Behind it was some sort of railway station, but I didn't find that out until the morning. Sadly, that was information I could have used before checking in.

Through the tinny air duct, I could hear the wheezing and other bodily functions of the two twenty-something men in the next room with surprising clarity. I took out an iced tea from the ice chest and watched from the window as one man hauled a couple of trash bags out of the back of a faded and old baby blue truck. Long brown hair swirled against his face as a small dust devil crossed his path before blowing out and falling back to earth. A brown cigarette hung from his bottom lip. No shirt, not a bad body, jeans torn at both knees and slung low enough to reveal a butt crack.

The wheezing in the next room was nothing compared to the noise coming from behind the motel. The next day I found out that the rail station was a freight station hub. It buzzed with activity all night. Every few minutes the room vibrated from an explosive crash that sounded like large cement blocks being thrown into big metal containers—but I wouldn't bother to investigate the next day. I hardly slept at all, but Steve heard nothing and looked puzzled when I mentioned it in the morning. "What noise?"

After some cereal and milk from the cooler, I drove south on 530 into Flaming Gorge. Near the border of Utah, I took a side road toward the lake for an early lunch. The air was so still and silent we found ourselves whispering. It was surprisingly desolate—only a couple of boats and a few fishermen were anywhere to be seen. We were surrounded by miles of knee-high scrub and flat pale rocks; whatever wildlife lived there would have to be short and beige. We ate tuna sandwiches and boxed juice, and I watched Steve hunt for lizards for a while until the heat and lack of shade got us back on the road.

Just north of Vernal, we found a campground in the Ashley National Forest called Red Canyon. The campsite was more like a camping resort. There was a lake and lodge with a dock, fishing, canoes, horseback riding, and hiking trails. I planned a sunrise hike on the Canyon Rim Trail, an easy ten miles along the rim.

"Hey, Mom. Canoes! Let's do it. I want my own."

"Okay, but let's set up camp first. But we're sharing a canoe. What if I fall in? I'm going to need you to haul me out."

"That lake looks pretty small. I think you could walk out."

I discovered the restaurant at the lodge had pork chops and mashed potatoes—real food, so I had to eat there. I was tired of my campfire cooking, cafe sandwiches, and pizza. At the lodge, plastic chairs sat on a large, organized deck overlooking the lake. I let Steve bring his Game Boy to dinner so I could have a scotch and sit in solitude for a few minutes. The bottom of the trees and grass near the water's edge disappeared into the yellow light of the sunset, and for a moment a fleeting sense of loneliness came over me. I stared at the lake with eyes unfocused and allowed it to hypnotize me with brief memories of still water and gentler times. My days were washing away, being poured out from a pitcher that seemed nearly empty.

The deck, with the still lake below and the quiet voices above, seemed like a place for lovers—even a bit of déjà vu from a weekend with Jason—but there were no young lovers.

On the deck were three older couples, probably retired, and

a small family group with an accent that sounded Dutch. Off the deck, a father and four blonde boys, all similar in age—quads maybe—with yellow life jackets walked all in a row, one after the other to the lake's edge, a daddy duck and his chicks. They pushed through the tall grass to a waiting canoe where they all tumbled and jumped on board with no thought to the balance requirements of a floating object. The canoe rocked side to side, making sucking sounds as it moved in the mud. Father duck spoke a few sharp commands and the chicks sat down immediately.

A man, sitting alone at the table next to me, struck up a conversation that quickly sunk into a dissertation on toilet technology due to his preference for the vault toilets at the campground. He was with the Park Service on a project to assess the toilets in the parks. Chuck was sitting with legs crossed at the knees. His shirt was a yellow and pink print and he had on deck shoes and khaki pants. His hair was slicked back, and he was a bit too tan. He looked like he belonged on his Van de Stadt sloop somewhere in the Caribbean—not here at a campsite in Utah assessing toilets.

He leaned toward me, elbow on his knee, "There are four kinds of toilets. There's a pit toilet, which means that it's a seat over a hole inside an enclosure, a flush toilet which we all know about, a chemical toilet, the standard port-a-potty type, and a vault toilet, which they have here."

"Really," I said, trying to be polite but not sound too interested.

I saw Steve's eyes look up from his Game Boy a few times, but he didn't join the conversation.

"...and then there's the vault toilet which is a private enclosure surrounding a hole in the ground which has a seat and standoff going into a cesspool. Evidently, the U. S. Forest Service designed the concept of SST or sweet-smelling toilet..."

Finally, the food came, and I was rescued.

. . .

I woke Steve just before 6 AM. "Ready for our hike? We're going to see the sunrise over the canyon, but we need to go now."

"How long is it?"

"Only ten miles up and back and mostly flat, but major views from the clifftop. An easy hike, but I'm hoping we're going to see some bald eagles and maybe some bighorn sheep, you know, the kind that cling to cliff sides? Oh, and we're on a cliff top, so don't screw with me by getting too close to the edge. If you fall off the cliff, there will be no ice cream for you at lunch."

He looked at me, chin down, eyes looking up and with sarcasm, "Gravity is a harsh mistress."

Dino-Mite

Vernal, Utah to Denver, Colorado

I pushed open the door of the Econo Lodge and breathed deep. Two overnight bags flew past me, each onto a separate bed.

"Hey Steve, watch out. I have some breakable stuff in my bag."

"I've seen the stuff in your bag. There are six pairs of shoes which I don't understand, hand lotion, a bottle of Excedrin, and a toothbrush. Oh, and contact lenses and some of that stuff you put on your eyelashes for some reason. So, freshen up or whatever you call it, and let's get outta here Pinky, I wanna see some dinosaur stuff."

We were excited to explore Vernal, the gateway to dino-everything and home to one of Utah's largest quarries of prehistoric Jurassic dinosaur bones, but first, we were hot and hungry. It was 11 AM and a debilitating 98 degrees. We had already walked ten miles at Red Canyon, so we stopped to eat and cool down at the 7/11 Ranch Cafe.

A large, petrified tree trunk stood in the center and a stuffed elk's head hung over a brick fireplace. His eyes were lifeless, but the rest of the place was alive with a friendly local ambiance. Just after I put in our order, a mid-fifties woman at the next table leaned over to Steve.

"Don't forget to see the *T. rex* at night. He's decorated for the fourth of July with a cowboy hat and scarf and covered in lights."

Steve's head looked up from a brochure he was reading, "There's a *T. rex* here? Cool. Where is it?"

"It's just down the street. Can't miss it. And there's a big pink brontosaurus on the other end of town, but the town likes to decorate the *T. rex* for all the various holidays. They put bunny ears on him at Easter."

"That's cute," I giggled. "You were here at Easter too?"

"Oh, we live here. My husband works at the Quarry Exhibit at the Dinosaur National Monument."

"What fun. We're going there tomorrow. Thanks for the tip."

Next morning, we took a drive down the street to see the *T. rex*, visited the Utah Field House of Natural History Museum and walked around the Dinosaur Garden, which had at least fifteen full-sized dinosaur replicas, none of which were in pastel colors. Somewhere in all that driving around town, we found a place called Hug-a-Pig, a little gift store market and a small petting zoo with several goats, pigs, and one particularly friendly Vietnamese potbellied pig. Steve and the pig had an instant bond. He asked to go back several times to visit him. We liked Vernal so much; we stayed another day.

With the giant pink cement brontosaurus in my rearview mirror, we headed for Dinosaur National Monument only thirty minutes east and just over the border with Colorado.

The Monument no longer includes the subtropical terrain that made up the late Mesozoic era, but it is an impressive display of 1500 dinosaur bones still embedded in the side of a mountain, now covered and protected inside the exhibit hall. Outside we walked about a half mile down the Fossil Discovery Trail, but it was too hot and there was no shade. It was the first time I'd seen Steve's face red with heat as he sat on a cement bench looking tired. We turned around and got back on the road. Next stop Steamboat where we hoped it would be a little cooler.

We breezed through a town called Dinosaur on Highway 40, also known as Brontosaurus Boulevard. It seemed to be no town at all, although a few houses and even fewer trees spread out over the arid landscape. The odd thought crossed my mind that I could buy a cheap plot of land and call it Dtown or Lynnville. My first order of business would be to ban all leaf blowers and pastel-colored dinosaurs.

One after another, old mining towns tumbled past. Many had been turned into tourist traps or ski resorts, all overdone and overpriced. Our first stop was in Steamboat Springs for lunch, which was like Jackson but with more overt luxury. After spending more money than necessary on a Native

American piece of pottery, we continued to Silverthorne where we would spend the night at the Alpen Hutte Hostel.

Silverthorne had no real walkable downtown, but there was plenty of commercialization, both natural and man-made. It appeared to be a crossroad—a stopover between bigger towns, ski resorts, and second homes and seemed to revolve around the outlet mall.

The hostel was clean and simple on the inside, but full of mostly local area travelers and giggling female shopping groups. The outside looked like a large gingerbread house from a fairy tale—faux-medieval style, or Tudor revival with the look of the half-timbering construction technique of the Middle Ages. It even had the large X in half-timbers. One of the many things I had an interest in but knew little about was symbology. If the timbers are crossed like the letter X, it symbolizes the cross of St. Andrew on which they crucified him.

We got up early and located coffee and chocolate milk before moving on toward Evergreen and into Denver. I took Loveland Pass because I remembered it as a kid. I recalled how my brother and I used to get on the floor of the old hunchback army-green Chrysler because looking out the window was too scary.

At nearly 12,000 feet, Loveland Pass is one of the highest mountain roads in Colorado with many hairpin curves and dangerous drop-offs. Plus, there are other hazards, the height can cause some people altitude sickness and there is less oxygen for car engines which can cause a stall, and always the possibility of snow or hazardous weather even in summer. As the driver, you can't see much because you can't take your eyes off the road—you have to pull over at an overlook to wonder at the massive landscape of pink, purple, and gray captured in a million paintings.

We stopped for a break at the Arapahoe Basin Ski area. To my amazement, there were cars in the lot and people skiing. It was mid-July.

Steve, not usually impressed by majestic panoramas, was interested and curious, "How high are we?"

"Almost 11,000 feet right here, but the summit is over 13,000 feet. Do you see where the trees start to thin out toward the top? That's the tree line or some say timber line."

I remember being fascinated as a kid when my father spoke so confidently of the forest and the timberline. "That's the altitude where trees stop growing. There's not enough oxygen for them," he said. "They can't breathe."

"Colorado has fifty-some mountain peaks higher than 14,000 feet—the most of any state. I wonder how they measure a mountain. We should find out. I think it involves sea level and some sort of math."

"Mom, do you know what the highest mountain in the world is?"

"Everest, of course."

"No," he smiled. "It's Mauna Kea."

"Hawaii? No."

"It's true. When my dad and I were in Maui, a kid at the hotel told me his dad and mom just hiked it and it's the tallest if you start counting at the base which is under the ocean."

"What? Really? That's a trick question."

"It's true. Can we go skiing?"

There wasn't enough snow to do much of anything, and the crowds were thinning out. After a half-hour throwing slushy dirty snowballs at each other, we continued toward Evergreen Lake, where I remembered ice skating as a kid, and then stopped at Red Rocks Amphitheater so we could run up and down the steps for a bit of exercise. We were only a couple hours from Denver.

Seeing Denver would be a step back in time. I was born there, but the summer after my eleventh birthday we moved to Southern California. Memories were vague. I remember my brother said he saw an alien craft hovering over our backyard one Sunday morning as we got ready for church. He was seven years old. I was nine. Although our parents dismissed his claims as illusions, I secretly hoped it was true. Without the hope of alien antics, I worried Denver would be a place no one bothered to describe—unremarkable, a place where everything important was accomplished somewhere else.

It was there I stretched out on summer clover with my

friend Sylvia to envision images in clouds. It was there I first wore pantyhose and learned about the mechanics of sex from a porn paperback found behind a dumpster (which cleared up the whole people-made-babies-in-bathwater thing).

Somewhere around the age of ten, I realized my childhood was turned on its ear. My father was the pastor at a Jehovah's Witness church, but they didn't call it a church and they didn't call him a pastor. They had different names, rituals, and rules, and even a different Bible. It wasn't until many years later that I realized their Bible was different or that I had never been vaccinated or been to a doctor, except for the dog bite incident.

The impact of those differences was realized when I was treated as an outcast as soon as I started school, but it took many years for me to understand why anyone, including some teachers, would be mean to me—a petite five-year-old who was so shy I sat in the back of the classroom and rarely spoke. How did they not like someone so invisible as me?

By the time we moved to Southern California, I had cleared up a few things in my head. I was young but had come to some realizations about my life. I knew my mother would be no help at all navigating girl-teen territory. And I also knew I would reject their religion.

By the time I was eighteen, the rejection would be absolute. I wouldn't just reject parts of that religious doctrine; I would reject it all—all organized religion. It wasn't until I was in my late twenties that I realized my upbringing had some benefits. I became independent and self-sufficient early, refusing to rely on others or take things at face value. I had to search for truth. I had to discover my own abilities and self-worth. I questioned people, places, motives—everything. I didn't believe I was entitled, that a god was there to protect me or help me or that I deserved some grand future more than anyone else. I became solidly pragmatic. Show me the science. Show me the logic.

My obsession with raising my son with truth and reality was a direct result of the attempts to square the circle of my life. It required the slow and methodical unraveling of childhood religious constraints and a reconfiguration of my thoughts about men, family, community, and a future where I didn't believe the world was ending every day.

I tapped the laptop to get Steve's attention. "Tomorrow we're going to see if we can find my old house where I used to live as a kid."

"Was it a cool house?"

"It was just a house, nothing fancy. I'm curious about what it looks like these days. Not sure I can find it. I don't know the full address. Where do you want to go afterward? There's a zoo, aquarium, an amusement park, and there's the Denver Mint, or go-kart racing. Or we can go to the botanical gardens or an art museum or walk around downtown shopping and eating ice cream."

The reply was instant, "Go-karts and then ice cream."

The next day, I found the house. It had been moderately remodeled on the outside, but I recognized it from the neighborhood. I remembered the way the house sat on the corner lot. I recognized the house across the street where I had an instant memory of the pretty high school girl who came home from skiing one day with blisters all over her red puffy face from sun poisoning. I remembered the chain-link fence on the other side of the street that once contained a noisy little black and white dog, and I remembered the way the houses to the east were spread out bigger and grander than our little bungalow.

There was Denver now—all grown up. It had moved on as I had and become a place of remarkable achievements and profound personal memories.

Sitting on a bed at a Denver Econo Lodge, twisting my head to peer through the curtain-folds to monitor the drug dealers in the room four doors down, I looked over to beam silently at my sweet son. He was drawing something on a pad of Post-its. It was a *T. rex* flipbook.

Road Noise

Trucker Trouble

North Platte to Lincoln, Nebraska

Hundreds of flies blackened the window of a gas station outside of North Platte, trying to cool off their tiny fly feet. It was 6 PM and 105 degrees.

Stepping out of the car into the motel parking lot, I could feel my contact lenses curl up. Steve's face was red with heat as he hurried me so he could get into the pool. The pool wasn't much to see, a rectangle of water contained in concrete. Plastic chairs, no umbrellas. Chain-link.

Flat yellow grassland surrounded us. North, south, east, west—it all looked the same. Across the highway, a few clumps of trees offered little relief to the cows huddled in the cracked mudhole underneath.

Within minutes after check-in, we were poolside. Six kids of assorted sizes and colors jumped and laughed in the roadside motel pool. A baseball-size frog attempted to join them in a desperate search for water. Steve tried to save him from a chlorine death by hand-delivering him back to the field just over the chain-link fence. He carried him like a fresh egg held delicately cupped in his palms, then pushed the frog through a gap at the bottom of the fence and shooed him away. Within thirty minutes, the frog was back at the edge of the chemical lake. As Steve picked him up again, the frog let out little squeaky sounds like a stuffed toy—not the *ribbit* sound of cartoons. I wondered how long he would survive; would he die of thirst beyond the fence, get sucked into the chlorinated pool filter overnight, or would a hawk swoop down on him tomorrow just after the little guy found a drink at the cow's mudhole? For a split second, I pondered the delicacies of the circle of life.

Steve was talking to the frog this time as he carried him back to the fence. He had gathered a following of three children. They all pounded the fence to scare the frog back to the lifeless yellow wilderness just beyond. We didn't see him again.

It is impossible to miss the spotlessness of Nebraska. Even the haystacks line up in neat rows. Perhaps it is the neatness, the predictability of their mere presence that's soothing and troubling at the same time. The visualization of continuity—row after row, shape after shape, year after year—always the same. Even the roads are straight, the mailboxes lined up and the houses similar in size and color—variations of off-white and the palest of yellows. Then, every few miles there would be some small divergence from the conformity—perhaps an act of heroism—a red door, a pig-shaped mailbox, or ugly gnomes behind a little white decorative fence. There was just enough variation to support a declaration of individuality.

Steve pointed out a variety of haystacks we saw in the fields along the road. Small rectangles seem to be popular in certain areas. In others, there were bread-loaf-shaped stacks—the ones we saw most often in Nebraska. The bread loaves were usually stacked on top of one another, I assume to conserve space; but the loaves fell apart with rain and wind, turning them into sleeping golden elephants. Then there were the actual stacks, the kind seen in fairy tales and kids' books. Neatest of all were the hay rolls. They also appeared to morph into elephants, but in the interim, they spread out across the fields like plump crepes browning in the sun.

In the early morning hours on Interstate 80 east of North Platte, I had a confrontation with a trucker driving an eighteen-wheeler. We were alone on the divided highway when I tried to pass him, but every time I tried, he blocked me weaving into the left lane speeding up, and then slowing his truck again after I backed off. He would do that several more times slowing down to invite me to pass then speeding up.

At first, I didn't think much of it, assuming he had some reason to do that, but during my fourth attempt to pass he let me get halfway alongside his truck before moving to the left as if to run me off the road. I had to apply the brakes to get away from him. It was at that point I realized he was screwing with me, and I was suddenly furious. I could see him smile in his side mirror, and I'm sure he thought he would get away with it.

I had to drive fast to catch up to the truck to see all the information on the back, including the phone number for dispatch to report his bad driving. *What an idiot.* I told Steve to get out a piece of paper and write down the numbers on the back of the truck. Steve had already noticed that I was tense, and that there was some sort of problem with the truck in front of us.

"What's going on Mom?"

"I have to keep my hands on the wheel, so I need you to do something. On the back of that truck, there's a phone number and a truck number; write them both down and the plate number. Let me know when you got it."

He didn't hesitate and a few seconds later said, "I got the numbers."

"Now dial that number, wait for an answer, and then hand me the phone."

As soon as he handed me the phone, I backed off my speed, but stayed close behind the truck. A second later, I put the cell phone to my left ear and looked straight at the trucker in his side mirror. He saw me and I saw his face change from that arrogant smile to fearful surprise. He hadn't just harassed anyone on the road; he had poked a mother bear, cub in the car, with a cell phone in 1995. And the Verizon coverage in the middle-of-nowhere-Nebraska was excellent.

Instantly, he slowed down and pulled over to the right and off the road to a stop. I stayed with him, pulling off the road, but keeping a suitable distance behind him. I stayed in my car as I spoke to the dispatcher, telling him his trucker tried to run me and my son off the road. I was so angry my voice was shaking. I told him the truck number and our location, and the dispatcher was quick to assure me he would take care of it. He told me to stay on the phone with him while he called the truck. In the meantime, the trucker had gotten out of the truck and was walking around his eighteen-wheeler examining his tires. *Did he think I was falling for that?* A few seconds later, I could tell a call had come into the truck as the driver quickly moved to the cab. Less than a minute later, the dispatcher came back on the phone.

"I've spoken to the driver, and I can assure you ma'am you will have no more problems with this truck."

My voice was angry and loud, "I'm going to pull out now, but if I ever, and I mean ever, see this truck in my rearview mirror, I will call the State Patrol and then I'll call my lawyer."

I didn't actually have an on-call lawyer, but it sounded like something I should say at the time.

"I assure you ma'am you will never see him again."

I pulled out and onto the highway and glanced repeatedly for a long time in my rearview mirror. I never saw the truck again.

The next day, a visit to the Folsom Children's Zoo in Lincoln started dramatically as I locked the keys in the car. It was 10 AM and 105 degrees as I crouched in the shade of the Blazer waiting for the locksmith while Steve shopped in the air-conditioned gift store. I was hot and angry and had convinced myself that I was in for a rip-off and cursed again my need to self-impose timelines that cause me to rush things. Money was tight. I had a strict budget for this trip, and I had not figured-in acts of stupidity that would cost me money. I prepared myself for a gas surcharge and a having-to-come-out-in-the-heat surcharge and most definitely, a helping-an-idiot-tourist surcharge. But twenty minutes and $25 later, I was inside the gift shop having ice cream with Steve. I regretted my poor attitude and made it up to myself by buying him a stuffed monkey. After that event, Steve must have asked me 150 times over the rest of the trip if I had the keys before he shut his door.

The sun was peeking through the tree behind me, and little laser beams were hitting my shoulders. I pushed myself further left on the bright yellow child-size bench to move out of the sun. Steve appeared from the massive plastic play structure—a giant gerbil maze in all the primary and secondary colors. I watched Steve pass some strangers sitting on a parakeet-green mini bench about twenty yards away. I speculated they were the parents of a child that was also playing in the maze. He passed them and then stopped and walked backwards to them. He stopped in front of them and turned toward them like a robotic superhero. He seemed to ask them about the toy the woman had in her lap. I couldn't hear the conversation, but I could read his animation. He was chattering away, making gestures with his hands, and it all seemed to be related to the toy. They laughed and shook his hand. He started to run back to the playground when they called him back. They handed him something. I found out later it was money.

It was money from Italy. They were from a small town near Naples visiting relatives, and it seemed they had a stuffed gecko they were holding for their nephew. Steve's conversation was about the gecko because he had a real one at home being babysat during our trip.

Throughout the trip he freely talked to strangers and if they had an accent, he would ask them where they were from and tell them he was collecting money. At first, I cringed and wondered if I should not allow the money solicitations, but then decided not to worry about it. Everyone seemed to enjoy him and happily reached in pockets to add a few foreign coins to his collection. By the end of the trip, he had met people and collected coins from eighteen countries from as far away as Australia and Africa.

Road Noise

Bridges Nowhere

Winterset, Iowa

Grassy flat, two-dimensional fields were morphing into rolling manicured farms. The transition from Nebraska into Iowa landscape was distinctive.

Every few miles a corn co-op on one corner and a church on the other reminded me that this was Middle America; a place with illusions held tight. It's not the America I know; people care about different things yet still, time passes, and old ideas and beliefs become dinosaurs that can't adapt and will die out. I had this idea about the Midwest, this stereotype of brave determination based on many disparate religious ideologies where the primary goal was to maintain the status quo. *But which ideology? Which status quo? Which god?*

Despite those thoughts, I predict more people from the congested, overpriced, arrogant west will move there to spend more time porch-sitting so they can spread their arms without touching another person as they reluctantly fall into their senior years.

Steve was on the computer playing a game. He was not

interested in mile after mile of rolling farmland or small-town architecture. Although I continued to point out cows in the field or an escaped chicken wandering roadside, I was just entertaining myself. He was, however, interested in all nature of roadkill, gagging smells of the pastures, and cheap roadside amusements with gift shops.

My goal was Winterset and the covered bridges, so I got off the Interstate and followed several straight nameless narrow roads passing farm after identical farm. On one long, straight, quiet road where nothing was moving except a lone tractor in a golden field, I asked Steve if he wanted to drive. In a few months, he would be twelve and he was already nearly as tall as me, with longer legs and a sharper mind, so I wasn't worried. I let him drive for quite a while as I searched the map to find the location of one of the covered bridges, but without road signs and street names, the map was of little use. Thanks to the compass in the car, I just kept heading east.

He drove confidently, his long legs reaching the pedals with no problem. His eyes swept the landscape and back to the road as if he had an instinct for driving like he had for people mentally matching observations against possibilities, words against action.

Winterset was a charming town that found unexpected fame and took advantage of it. Who could blame them? In 1992, *The Bridges of Madison County* came out as a book and then, just before our trip, the movie. It brought with it a reverence for idealized love, the illusion of men who appreciate romance and the intimacy of old covered bridges. Of course, old, covered bridges usually have bats in the rafters, creaky planks, and peeling paint—but then so do fantasy lovers.

The story is—lonely middle-aged homemaker meets aging world-traveling photographer, culminating in four days of lusty passion. But then what? What I loved about the movie, and I think others did too, were the lovers. They were not beautiful young Hollywood things—they were everybody else, stodgy bored housewife and balding loner. Lover, Robert was a reminder that traditional masculinity was dying in the 1980s and passion-starved Francesca, a reminder that martyrdom (*or is it admirable loyalty?*) was still alive and well. But we loved the romantic dialogue; Robert's famous line, *"It seems right now that all I've ever done in my life is making my way here to you."* Or *"I don't want to need you, because I can't have you."* Sweet. Class-act romance simplified to life in the shadow of an aging covered bridge.

Until I told him about the bats in the rafters, Steve was mostly uninterested as I explored four of the six bridges in the area, and he tried to spot a bat. To me, they were just bridges—picturesque landscapes, old and mostly rundown until movie fame plagued the area with plein-air artists and camera-toting tourists from every country. The fame of the town was still young on our arrival. Only the Roseman had installed a simple gift shop. A jolly middle-aged man in overalls provided a smile and friendly greeting and an offer of a soda and traveler's conversation on the wooden rocking chairs on his porch.

If there was a romance about Winterset, I didn't feel it, but to be fair, I wasn't much in a romantic mood. Life in Winterset would be too simple for me. Francesca finally realized the complexity of life outside her small town, and it scared her. I was hoping she would pull that door handle and run for Robert's truck. But then, that's where all this started—with all my impulsive decisions about men and idealized romance. My life would have been better, or at least more consistent and tamer had I been the levelheaded Francesca.

We spent the night at the Village View Motel off Highway 92, where I discovered my laptop had a problem. I could only see half of the screen.

The computer was still under warranty. It surprised me how fast I got hold of Toshiba support that night. They said a graphic chip had come loose or failed and I could take it to the nearest support center, and they would fix it no problem.

"Well, actually, there's another problem," I said. "I'm on a road trip across the country for three months. I'm currently in Iowa, but I'm leaving tomorrow for Chicago."

"That sounds exciting," he said. "That's not a problem. It will take us a few days to get the chip. Where will you be in three days?"

I was impressed. What could have been a major problem, Toshiba solved in minutes. For free.

Summer in the City

Chicago, Illinois

Cows huddled under skinny clumps of trees that spread over mudholes, still damp courtesy of center pivot irrigation. At this time of day, the pivots stood dry and quiet in the fields. It was nearly noon and the mudholes were now just cracked, damp dirt. The empty brown eyes of the cows stared out between fence posts. Tails flipped and flies hovered, but there was only a whisper of wind. It was hot. Really hot. I reluctantly turned on the radio to get the news. One intent of the trip was to avoid as much television, radio, and newspapers as possible. Besides bad news, sensationalized journalism (I had long ago developed a mistrust of the media), and the trite ramblings of young perky-breasted newscasters, I was trying to reconstruct some optimism about life, so it seemed counterproductive to spend any time at all reading the news. I figured if nuclear war was imminent, a friend would call my cell and give me a heads-up so I could grab some Excedrin, lip gloss, and a sweatshirt and find an overturned school desk where Steve and I could take shelter.

The interior temperature gauge on the car console was

reading 113 degrees. Heat-monkeys radiated off the road and the inside of the car was hot despite the blasting air conditioning. There was a heat wave throughout the Midwest, and we were only miles from the heart of it—Chicago, July 15, 1995.

When we arrived in Chicago, I realized the extent of the heat wave—the worst ever in the region. There were power outages throughout much of the city—hospitals were overrun, and hotels were taken up by locals. After two hours of driving and calling around, I found a Howard Johnson's that had rooms and I soon found out why—they didn't have air conditioning. But the room faced into a hint of a breeze and wide glass doors opened out to the pool.

Everyone was in the pool. Doors to the rooms facing the pool were standing open and people sat in entryways fanning themselves wearing as few clothes as possible. Standard rules didn't apply. Guests roamed the halls with cold beers and bare feet—men, big-bellied and bare-chested and women strolling in swimwear letting flabby arms fly against the heat.

Steve headed for the pool, and I picked a spot under an awning-covered table with my iced tea and book, *The Self-Aware Universe*, exploring one of my favorite subjects—consciousness. I prefer to believe we live in a universe where everything is interconnected at a fundamental matter level; what we observe, we affect, and that consciousness exists outside matter. I am not talking about god—just pure energy without interest in our personal lives, sports teams, politicians, or attendance at fractured-light, song-filled churches.

Three local twenty-something men had decided to make a party of the heat wave and had jumped the hotel fence with their cooler full of beer. They were already hammered when I met them and spent the afternoon taking quick dips in the pool, pounding more beers, and flirting with every female in the immediate vicinity. They were not picky. Although I was young looking for my age, I was still well over theirs.

While Steve shared pool games and energetic company with a group of children around his age, I shared a beer with the fence jumpers. They turned out to be younger than I thought; still in college, all at Loyola. Two were pursuing computer science degrees and the other, Kevin, a theoretical physics major.

Kevin pointed a finger at my book, "I just finished reading that. What do you think?"

"Well, I just started reading it, but I think if we can get enough people to understand our common consciousness, it may be the only way we will survive as a species. Our self-absorbed worldview that we are all separate is destroying us."

"Do you think that will happen?"

"I'm not an optimistic person but I'm trying."

Kevin grinned exposing dimpled cheeks and perfectly aligned upper-class white teeth and for the next hour and through an alcohol and heat filtered haze, Kevin and I explored the ideas of the elements of reality, the existence of physical matter, and the possibility of transcendent dimensions. I admit he was way over my head in truth and theory, but I tried to keep up with what little I knew about quantum mechanics.

"Individual separateness is an illusion," said Kevin while smiling at me. "Carl Jung believed that there is a transpersonal collective aspect of our unconscious. I believe it operates outside space-time and we can recognize it when an event in the outside world coincides meaningfully with a psychological state of mind. Synchronicity."

"So, you're saying there's essentially this mysterious connection between our psyche and the material world, and that fundamentally they are only different forms of energy?"

"Exactly," he said. "We experience synchronicity when we are thinking of something, and then, almost immediately, we notice something else that seems to have a meaningful connection to what we were just thinking or feeling. Have you ever had that happen?"

His youthful face grew more handsome as I heard him speak, and I wished I were twenty years younger.

"Yeah, I think so," I said. "I remember once I was rafting with some friends, and I was tossed out of the boat into class three rapids. I was terrified and struggled to calm myself and connect with the water instead of fighting against it. Suddenly a dragonfly hovered in front of me for the longest time, and I found myself mesmerized by it. It flew in small circles like it was calling me, trying to connect to me and pull me toward the outstretched hands that were waving to me from the raft. I felt a calmness come over me and then I easily swam back to the raft."

"Exactly," he said. "An exceptional experience. That connection—that dragonfly hovering in front of you delivered a meaningful message to illuminate exactly what you needed at that time. And it shows we're not just connected to other people; we're connected to every living thing."

"Some people want to just think of it as coincidence, but if people would only allow themselves to believe…"

We were interrupted by Steve who claimed he was hungry. It was time for me to leave—back to my reality. We found a nearby Denny's to eat and wait out the trip to the airport to pick up a friend who would join us for a few days.

After we couldn't drag out dinner at the air-conditioned Denny's any longer, I decided we would go to the airport early. At least it would be cool there, except that heat-related issues had delayed her flight for two hours—so we had nearly four hours to wait. Steve managed to curl up in an airport chair and sleep. I put my purse behind my neck on the rigid back of an airport row-chair and dozed for ten-minute intervals until my mouth dropped open and I woke myself up snoring. After a few times, I realized I was too self-conscious to continue that public sleeping display. I got another coffee and people watched.

There was the usual assortment—generic salesmen in ill-fitting suits, pudgy twenty-something women in stretch denim shorts and too-tight T-shirts with an iron-on photo of a Shih Tzu, and moms pushing strollers packed with tote bags of toys and two kids in tow eating cinnamon rolls as big as their heads. Sitting next to me was a forty-something man with graying hair, baggy cargo pants, a lot of stubble, and a Kurt Cobain T-shirt. He half-smiled and nodded when I looked his way. I sensed he was about to start-up a conversation. I was not in the mood for a debate about the importance of Cobain in pushing synth pop culture out the window. I didn't really care for the shouting anguished lyrics, but I did understand his dread of living in world so apathetic.

I moved next to Steve across the aisle, still sleeping bent and curled across two chairs and stroked his shaggy hair.

He stirred, "Stop. I'm trying to sleep."

Although most airport crowds are generally unattractive, Chicago is not. After many business trips, it had become my favorite airport and big city. If I could stand the wind and winters, if I were twenty years younger, and if I had some fascinating big city occupation, I would live there, preferring its intellectual complexity to the chaotic artsiness of New York City. *Ah yes. Tailored, intrepid, and civilized men in white shirts were all over the Chicago airport.*

I looked at my friend dragging through baggage claim. She looked like she'd been beaten up, but she often had that look. Tara was a fighter—a gutsy girl with attitude who could talk the air right out of a room. She had a way of exhausting me with conversation to the point where I'd have to pass her to a friend while I went to bed. I'd known her for many years, and despite our different personalities and ultimate life goals, we appreciated each other's energy.

She was wearing khakis, a plain blue T-shirt, and Capezio flats. She carried two trendy, but not matching small bags that would be precisely packed and a real Coach purse. A faded blue Gap hoodie was tied around her waist. It must have been hot on the plane, or she would have been wearing the sweatshirt. We were always cold. We had determined that a sweatshirt was one of the four necessities in case of a disaster of any type—earthquake, tsunami, alien attack—whatever. On the way out the door—tropical tsunami bearing down—grab a sweatshirt, hand lotion, lip gloss, and Excedrin. Life without the Big Four in a Mad Max world—would be unbearable.

Road Noise

The Bomb Threat

Detroit, Michigan

It was nearly 9 PM when we arrived on the outskirts of Detroit. Tara, Steve, and I had walked, shopped, and ate Chicago for two hot days, often having to stop and sit down somewhere just to get out of the sun. Sweaty and tired, we were desperate to find a motel, preferably an Econo Lodge, the motel chain I found most consistent across the US. No luck.

Steve had to use a bathroom and Tara finally demanded we just stay at the next place—whatever it looked like. The next place was the Metropolitan Inn in Romulus, Michigan. It seemed to be in the airport flight path, but all cheap motels were either on a flight path or next to a railway station. The outside was rundown, and the area seemed iffy, but we were tired.

Instincts told me to take precautions with the car. This was the first place I put a lock on the steering wheel. I still had concerns about the contents of the car, particularly the bikes on the back, even though they were locked on individually and locked together with two intertwined Kryptonite locks. After we checked in and I determined where the room was located,

I went back outside and backed the car into a space directly outside our room window. I backed it up so far that the bicycles on the back touched the wall outside our window. Still, I would sleep restlessly and for good reason. It was at lunch the next day I realized that my spare tire had gone missing.

Each cheap motel room had its peculiarity. In one, the air conditioner made a loud regular thump every few minutes and vibrated the windows, providing a symphony of hum-thump that persisted the night—but at least we were cool. In another place, the pressure from the shower could blast your skin off or in another, you were lucky if the water stayed hot during the duration of a quick shower. In another, the sink didn't drain, or the towels were the size and consistency of dish rags. In another, the water smelled funny or didn't seem to wash off. It was always something. The Metropolitan Inn had all those irritations and a few others.

The lobby was run down with old broken furniture and no frills, but that didn't bother me. I felt a moment of relief at the sparse furnishings, glad no one was sleeping in the lobby and loud music wasn't bursting through the walls. We made our way down a darkish hallway and even in the dim light I could see the stains and wear on the carpet. When we opened the door to the room, we were immediately hit by a strong smell of mildew. We thought of leaving, but it was late and dark, and we didn't know where we were and decided we were better off in motel hell than wandering the roads of Romulus at midnight.

Tara and I assessed the room. The carpet was so dirty I didn't want to walk on it in my shoes. The blankets on the bed were a chemical anomaly—stiff and yet threadbare at the same time, but they looked clean. The towels were the size of tea-towels with frayed edges. There were several disturbing stains on the single fabric chair in the room, but those were mostly obscured by the 1950s flower pattern.

"I'm not walking on this barefoot," Tara said.

"I have a procedure for places like this—although this is the worst I've ever seen. Grab that side." I motioned to the other side of one of the two bedspreads. "Now we flip it and lay it inside up between the beds."

"Inside up?" She laughed as she quickly picked up on my plan and we both grabbed the edges of the other bedspread.

"Usually, I put this one between the bed and the bathroom."

We were hysterically laughing now as we flipped over the second bedspread onto the rust-colored crusty shag carpet.

Steve, familiar with my routine, patiently waited for me to inspect his bed before jumping in—dirty clothes, shoes, and all. He would get a bed to himself as always, and Tara and I would share the other. None of this phased him. He was already opening the bag of dill pickle-flavored potato chips we found at a local market—something we had never seen. He was so impressed he entertained us with his version of television commercials for his newly discovered treat.

Tara and I walked around inspecting and commenting on the state of the room's filth. It was also freezing, so we turned off the air conditioner only to discover that the noise of it served more to drown out the airplanes directly overhead than to cool the room.

I insisted Steve sleep in his sleeping bag that night and not use the room's blankets—so that only left us with one sleeping bag between us and forced Tara and me to sleep directly on the bed's sheets, which meant we didn't sleep well.

We woke early and immediately began to laugh as we took a fresh look at the room in the light of day. Tara braved the shower first—which had decent pressure and hot water. While she showered, I called the front desk to request a couple more pint-sized towels, and I thought perhaps I would even force Steve to take a shower. After calling the housekeeping extension twice and getting no answer, I buzzed the reception desk. A woman's voice finally came on the line. In broken English, she said she was sorry, but couldn't give me more towels because the maid left.

She continued, "There's been threat. You leave now."

"What kind of threat?" I asked, and without waiting for her to answer, I asked another. "When were you planning on telling the guests?"

She mumbled something about a bomb and seemed distressed. I didn't bother with any more questions. I was already hanging up and yelling to Tara to get out of the shower.

"Steve! Get up. We need to leave quickly. Get your stuff together and hurry. Now, now, now!"

Tara was already out of the shower and pulling on clothes over her wet body and looking confused.

"Something about a bomb threat to the building," I said.

"Let's just get out of here!"

She was already throwing what few items we had brought in into anything container-like, and Steve was hustling, too. Within two minutes we were out of the building. I pulled the car out of the driveway, and we started to laugh. Steve was still half asleep and didn't know quite what had happened. Tara's hair was dripping wet, but clean and I had on the sweats I slept in.

"Niiiice place," Tara laughed.

"Classy, huh? Let's find a real breakfast place. I need coffee and I am going in like this—sweats, flip-flops, and unbrushed teeth."

I am sure Detroit has a sunny side, but the side we saw driving in was disturbing. The streets were mostly desolate, gray, and dirty with boarded-up windows where torn sheets hung like curtains and barbed wire fences guarded daycare centers. On every block, a couple of children played in a dirty courtyard. There were no children on bicycles or toys strewn on stoops, just cautious faces playing quietly near broken-down steps and piles of trash.

There were no twenty-somethings in jogging shorts and headphones, no old men reading on park benches, no yoga people sitting cross-legged meditating under a broad tree, and no children laughing and running on the spiky yellow grass of a corner park. Suspicious faces questioned our presence, and eyes that followed us down the street were telling us to leave.

We hurried to the Canadian border. One entrance sits in Detroit's downtown—the Detroit-Windsor Tunnel. In an instant the air seemed cleaner, curb-side beer bottles and plastic bags disappeared from the streets and buildings rose up at the side of the road delivering us to the good nature of our quiet little brother, Canada. No matter how many times we short-sheeted his bed, put rubber roaches in his cereal, or made fun of his lisp, he still smiled and shared his toys.

What a difference the Detroit-Windsor Tunnel makes, eh?

Squeeze Over!

Toronto, Canada

We were still in the Detroit-Windsor Tunnel when we began to call each other 'hoser', which I don't think they actually say in Canada. That was followed shortly by adding 'eh' to the end of every sentence. Not very original but blame it on Bob and Doug McKenzie.

The road to the city was a spotless highway with signs that asked us to *squeeze over*—so much more whimsical and polite than demanding we *merge*.

Toronto is like any other big city; traffic congestion, no place to park, and unless you stay a year, you can only taste a tiny kernel. There are the usual; people asking for handouts— some of the youngest I've ever seen—street entertainers, spiky-haired teens wearing dog collars, sleek-dressed ladies with too much makeup for such a hot day, women in hijabs and men in yellow plaid shorts carrying bags for round women in tight floral tank tops.

There was also a distinct concentration of tall, fair, and attractive men—an older, friendlier Venice Beach crowd, but with classier clothes. I wondered if most of the men were gay—too thin, single, and neat to be straight? I didn't have a problem with gay, I just liked stylish men and wished more of them would be hetero.

Before we did anything, we found the Toshiba Service Center to drop off my laptop to fix the dead chip. Two days later I picked it up—no problem, no hassle, no charge.

Steve wanted to go to Ontario Place, a recreation area—rides, shopping, IMAX—the usual generic entertainment. Tara insisted on the Hockey Hall of Fame. I wanted to shop, have a cocktail and people-watch from a sidewalk cafe. We did it all and didn't see that much of Toronto over the course of two days. Whatever impressions were made were trite and based on nothing but fleeting glances at nameless strangers, items in shop windows, types of debris on the sidewalk, and overheard fragments of conversations at nearby tables.

The Amsterdam Brewhouse on the waterfront brought back memories of the Crow's Nest in Santa Cruz sitting on the patio looking out at the ocean with some romantic partner. I was feeling my age—a forty-something—an hourglass with sand falling to the bottom, waiting for a turn to start again. I was on the other side of the age timeline now and still with so much left to do. I looked at Tara, her petite frame, and diaphanous features as she rattled on for fifteen straight minutes about the caretaking of her apartment in San Francisco, the social upkeep of numerous friends in multiple cities, states, and countries, and her intriguing neighbor on the third floor who she thinks is a drag performer at The Stud Lounge in the Castro. I couldn't keep up with the content, but I supplied an ear while intently absorbing the view of the young couple two tables over in a passionate kiss. I tuned back into Tara's voice. That was not the first time I had to filter out much of Tara's monologue. In a phone call one evening the only words I uttered were at the beginning and the end, 'Hi, what are you doing?' and 'Okay, talk to you later.' In the nineteen minutes in-between, she ranted about narcissistic bosses and San Francisco's spotty public transportation. Today, it was about her man-hating Women's Studies professor.

Tara leaned in, "Are you listening?"

"Yes. Yes, I heard. Why does the woman hate men so much? I get it, men can be pigs. So can women. Yes, women need to continue to fight for equality in all its forms, but those are political issues and to solve that we need more women in politics. Shouldn't we be focusing on the fundamental problem—equality in general instead of dividing people up into categories of color, culture, identity, and gender? Shouldn't it be less *I am woman hear me roar* and more *we are people, we are one*?"

"That's covered in sociology."

"Well, it's failing."

I suppose she agreed. She probably did but talking with Tara was often a one-dimensional conversation. It was hard to go deep with her and I love a good debate.

I was hoping for a more peaceful lunch but sitting on the waterfront brought back thoughts of my relationship disasters, perhaps because many started in the proximity of some large body of water while watching a deep orange sunset after a couple of margaritas.

Tara was quiet now and observing the kissing couple who were still going at it 20 minutes later, and then pointed to Steve, "Look."

Steve was about ten yards away talking to a couple with an invisible dog—that's a stiff leash constructed to look like a dog is at the end. Steve was going along with it and leaned down to pet the 'dog' causing the people at the next table to laugh and follow his lead by talking to the invisible dog. What a charmer he was—a personality trait I don't think I ever possessed.

"That's cute," said Tara. "What do you suppose an invisible cat would do?"

I laughed, "Flop over and just lay there on the ground?"

Shadow and Light

Watertown to Saranac Lake, New York
Burlington, Vermont

After dropping off Tara at the airport in Buffalo, we spent two days in Watertown sorting out technology issues and taking a rest from all the driving. In less than two weeks, Steve would be starting school on the road, and we needed to test the process of receiving and returning homework. The laptop screen issue had been resolved in Toronto—just a bad graphic chip. But the big problem was modem connection issues.

To send a fax from our motel rooms, we needed to use the modem in my laptop and connect it to the landline phone jack using an Ethernet cable. This was often unsuccessful and sometimes due to the *dial-9-for-an-outside-line* problem. I figured it was a modem settings problem, and after forty minutes on the phone with Megahertz tech support, I got it working—in most cases. There were still some places we stayed where it just wouldn't work. I assumed it was incompatibility with the phone system at that place. In those cases, I needed to use the cell phone hooked up to the laptop modem. That worked most of the time, unless the cell phone coverage was poor. I found it interesting that some of the oddest places had the best coverage. I remember receiving a phone call while we were hiking in the Adirondacks but having problems in Boston. I suppose it was due to cellular traffic in bigger cities. It was a challenge of the time. In 1995 the consumer Internet barely existed, and consumer Wi-Fi was still a few years away. Modems, like the one in my computer, were just beginning to pick up speed, but they weren't always compatible with every phone system. For the most part, I found it exciting to test out the technology in a real-life situation. I knew we were at the edge of a technology revolution, and although sometimes it was frustrating, I would literally jump up and down when it worked.

But sometimes it didn't work, and I had to stop at a local copy shop to send Steve's homework by old fashioned fax.

Her earrings wiggled and danced as she swung her head around to address me at the counter. A young woman with long brown hair and safety pins in her ears fiddled with the fax machine at a local copy center in Watertown, New York. Three pins were attached one to the other with three small purple glass beads at the bottom.

While I waited to send a fax, I asked if there was any significance to the earring design. She said her great-grandfather worked with Walter Hunt, a Watertown resident in the mid-1800s and inventor of the safety pin. She was re-creating pins as art—jewelry, clothing, wall hangings. My mind wandered as I envisioned all the things buckets of safety pins could be used for other than holding broken clothing together—limitless possibilities.

With our tech issues sorted, we drove straight to Saranac Lake with few stops. The landscape had the same green rolling hills, cows, and countryside that we had seen throughout Iowa and southern Illinois. In a picturesque little town called Harrisville, we stopped for lunch at the Hunter's View Cafe.

Steve was on the computer, as usual. He had discovered that he could record various mouth or armpit sounds and mix them with other recordings to form a full symphony of audio amusements. I soon stopped at a Walmart to buy him headphones. Of course, that only spared me the output, not the input.

From the direction of the passenger seat, I heard pig oink sounds. A few seconds later came laughter.

"You gotta hear this one, Mom."

. . .

Hazy sunbeams were hitting the forest floor, marking the path with layers of shadow and light on the slick stones. A shallow stream gurgled beside us, and the air still held drops from an early morning rain shower. As we walked, large drops fell on the leaves, making the forest wiggle and shimmer. The feeling was serene and yet claustrophobic. Each inhaled breath was thick and wet. A fragrant green blanket surrounded us, amplifying every tiny sound. A couple of times we heard a rustling in the trees. I thought perhaps a deer, but Steve was concerned about bears. Thankfully, neither appeared. We were near Tupper Lake, just outside of Saranac Lake.

I sat on a rock to rest and absorb the silence. Every few seconds water drops hit the top of my head, running down my cheeks and cooling my face. Steve was at the bank of the stream, poking a stick into the icy water. Tiny fish were everywhere, but he was poking at some large and slimy slugs, encouraging them to climb onto the stick for closer inspection.

After an hour on the trail, and with the late afternoon setting in, I decided we would turn back. Steve practically skipped back down the trail's slick rocks, pulling off our trail tags as he led the way back to the car without one wrong turn. I didn't call him to wait up—I was confident in his ability to navigate. He had been our map navigator from the start and did a great job considering many of the roads had no signs.

. . .

It was sunset at the Adirondack Motel at Saranac Lake. White Adirondack chairs lined up neatly on the lawn, and an older couple pumped their legs in a paddleboat on Lake Flower. We took a paddleboat out and when I couldn't move my legs anymore, Steve kept going. I felt tired and drained, but his energy continued well after dark. At 10 PM I calmed him down with tea and cookies and stargazing on the chairs outside overlooking the lake. We dipped cookies and toasted the end of the first thirty days of the trip.

Handicraft stores in upstate New York are as proliferous as fried food in Louisiana. We stopped at several. I was looking for a sock monkey, a throwback from my childhood. We never found the monkey, but Steve found a beaver.

"Look, Mom. A beaver! BEEAVERRRR!!" He exclaimed in a grandpa-voice holding the R sound at a higher pitch.

I recognized it immediately as grandpa from *Rocko's Modern Life*. If you are not familiar, Rocko is a wallaby. His best friend Hef is a cow that was adopted and raised by wolves. Hef's grandpa does not like wallabies, so he has been told that Rocko is a beaver, who grandpa takes great and frequent delight in harassing.

"I have to get this, it's our trip mascot!"

The beaver was a hand puppet, sort-of flat with a hand-hole, but it had a cute face and fit perfectly on the dash, which is where it sat the rest of the trip. Every so often, as Steve was getting into the car, he called out, 'BEAVERRRR!' I smiled every time.

It took an hour on the Port Kent ferry to cross Lake Champlain into Burlington. Only a few boats were on the water. Others, mostly skiffs and cruisers, quietly rocked in the marina, waiting for the afternoon sun and the beginning of the weekend.

I wandered the ferry and observed the diverse group of people making the crossing that Friday mid-morning. A slick-haired, dark-suited businessman talked on his cell phone the entire time. A twenty-something in khaki shorts dug into a navy-blue backpack for treats for a large curly-haired dog. A thirty-something guy in Madras shorts and thick-rimmed glasses posed for a picture being taken by a woman with long flaming-red hair wearing pink shorts and a cropped pink shirt—literally—she had cut off the bottom of the shirt. I looked for breasts poking out beneath but didn't see any.

Steve had wandered off and after a quick search, I found him leaning over the rail of the upper deck.

"Would you not do that? It makes me edgy."

"You're edgy anyway, Mom," he said with a smile.

"If you fall in, then I'd have to jump in, and you know how I hate cold water."

"Pinky, you're a threat to tolerance."

On the other side of the ferry ride sits Burlington, Vermont, a college town with the reconstructed charm designed-in by urban renewal city planners and market-savvy merchants. At the Church Street Mall, street vendors claimed space outside the pricey shops to sell T-shirts, hats, and ice cream. Coffee houses and outdoor cafes served tourists while street musicians played, and next-gen hippies danced on the mall. I found a bench and people watched while Steve explored the gift shops with the $20 I'd given him. I didn't figure the money would go far and expected him back for more.

A forty-something couple sat across the courtyard from me on a single bench. There was a sizeable gap between them, and they exchanged only a few words. *Hum*, there were rings on their fingers—probably married. I glanced at the man a few times. He looked familiar. *Did I know him?* I scanned my brain for some sort of file on him but didn't find one.

His expressionless face was looking down the mall past me at nothing in particular. Bored? Tired? Sad? His blonde wavy hair and long legs reminded me of an old friend. He must have felt my intrusion because his eyes looked at me and held my gaze. *Okay, maybe we knew each other—or maybe he's just a player—he looked so familiar.* He looked at me enough times that his wife finally looked in the same direction. She eyed me suspiciously. Suddenly she stood up and loudly stated, "We're going," and walked off. He obediently followed without protest and glanced at me as he walked away.

A man in short-shorts and a T-shirt with the short sleeves rolled up to his shoulders, showed off his weightlifter body as he chased his two-year-old down the brick courtyard. Another man with tattoos running up both arms and covering his neck was dressed all in black. He sat with his friends, frequently shook his long dark hair, and with animated hand gestures, apparently disagreed with much of their commentary.

After a day of people watching in Burlington, we took the backroads through the countryside and looked for a place to stay the night. There was a feeling of pseudo-suburbia—a calm and comfortable familiarity. Neat moderate pale houses all spread out in an organized pattern across textured fields and rolling meadows in every shade of green. Watercolor houses and gardens burst from clumps of sugar maple and beech trees, and small towns appeared every few miles—just often enough to provide a feeling of privacy and yet separateness all within a good shout from each another.

After several more stops at local craft and antique shops, I was beginning to hear complaints from Steve, and looked for a place to spend the night. We happened upon the Marsh-Plain Motel. It looked like a bed-and-breakfast and was perched on a rise above the road. Wildflowers surrounded a wide green lawn with waiting Adirondack chairs.

A friendly man greeted us inside and immediately asked if he could show his wife Molly my Blazer. They were in the market for an SUV and I was happy to point out my favorite features, particularly the overhead storage console with the outdoor temperature gauge and compass.

"That simple compass saved me from miles of needless driving due to many wrong turns on this trip!"

As they inspected my Blazer inside and out, I told them about our trip—three months around the US. They were curious and delighted and asked us a hundred questions. Then, they gave us the biggest room they had, a second-story apartment with its own porch overlooking the manicured lawn where croquet hoops waited. Their sixteen-year-old daughter asked Steve if he wanted to play croquet—and they did—well into the evening.

It may have been my first great night's sleep since the trip began. The air was cool and damp, and I snuggled into the deep softness of the country quilt and stayed for a while in the morning, listening for something familiar. Only birds and silence and Steve's deep breathing. I looked over at Steve's bed, but couldn't see him. He was under the quilt. Outside the window, a pinkish-gray mist hung over the meadow.

"Come on, Steve, let's get up. Molly is making us a pancake breakfast with real Vermont maple syrup they collect right here from these trees."

He must have been hungry because I didn't have to say it twice.

Just up the road we stopped at the Cabot Creamery, took a tour of the cheese-making facility, and bought a maple sugar candy moose. Back on the road, Steve played a game on the computer, and I enjoyed the hum of the highway, the misty morning, and the *Forrest Gump* CD.

Road Noise

Fire and Rain

Portland, Maine

The plan for this three-month trip was to drive three to four hours on most days. Most stops would be only for a day or two. We would leave early and arrive before noon. We spent the afternoons and nights exploring, hiking, visiting museums, national parks, sightseeing, or lounging by motel pools. Some days, things didn't go as planned.

It took longer than expected to get to Portland, Maine, since I tried to avoid the Interstates when possible. We arrived midafternoon. It was a day full of wrong turns and miles out of the way. Highway planners, or whoever oversees road signs, are not that meticulous about telling an out-of-towner where to turn. Often, highway signs give directions too late, or they were obstructed by trees or just confusing. Portland, Maine, was one of the worst.

I searched for quite a while for the Motel 6 where I had called in a reservation. I would have picked another motel except I had a package from Tom, Steve's father, and my ex-husband, waiting for me. The package was the video camera Tom loaned to me—and it came with a contract. Before the trip, everyone else I knew was anxious to loan me something without strings—camping equipment, fishing poles, coolers. But not Tom. For him, everything was a business deal, even during our marriage.

When I saw the box, I regretted telling him about the details of this trip and the association with Steve's school that I had titled *Virtual Classroom*. Although he was a VP at a tech company, his passion was to be a screenwriter and saw this trip—my trip—as an opportunity to turn it into a product. Although this trip was planned, organized, and financed by me, Tom had decided that somehow, we should mutually benefit.

About a month before we were to leave, Tom told me he had pitched an idea to his agent who had pitched it to a network who supposedly had an interest in our journey, so *'here is what I needed to do on the trip'*. He handed me a package of sketchy notes. More details and a contract were to follow with the video camera that he would send to me on the road.

I tried to avoid confrontation with him, but it never worked that way. He had a way of manipulating words. We had been divorced for nearly eight years, and I was still not saying *no* often enough. Communicating was impossible. Truth, facts, and logic, and what was best for our son, had nothing to do with it. My relationship with him was a balancing act, and for Steve's sake, I attempted to keep the peace but often failed.

Just seeing the box made me angry. I knew what to expect.

To me, the trip was a deeply personal project, a sabbatical, a private cleansing, a healing, and time to create a greater bond with my son. I never intended it to be a reality show. I didn't want someone following me and Steve with a camera and making me say things I didn't mean or endorse some purpose I didn't care about. The project was for me and Steve (even though he may not have understood all that). I wanted freedom. If we wanted to stop at a Vermont craft fair and look for sock monkeys or sit and people watch on a cobblestone street in Virginia or look for bats in the rafters of the Roseman Bridge, I wanted to do it because Steve and I had decided it— not because it was a staged and scripted performance.

Sitting on the bed at the Motel 6 in Portland, Maine, I read the contract and examined the camera. Why would I do it? I didn't think Steve even knew about this project of Tom's. And knowing Steve, he wouldn't want to do it, anyway.

"Steve, did you know your dad wants us to video some stuff from the trip—like scripted stuff for him and his agent? I don't want us to bother with that. Did you want to do it?

"Not really. What's it for, anyway?"

"Nothing we need to be concerned about. Okay, I was just checking. We're not doing it then."

Steve must have sensed a tone. "You seem mad."

"I just don't want to… I don't want to take time away from our trip to record some fake… some pretend events that might, in some off chance, be suitable for some advertiser or television program. This trip is not what that's about. I'm not mad, just frustrated, and tired. We drove too much today."

I felt the need to justify myself now and set expectations for Steve—or maybe for me. Steve was watching something on television and seemed wholly uninterested, yet I continued.

"Your dad wants us to do it, but I don't want to. I want to do just what we want to do on this trip. But he might be mad when we get back, you know."

"Mom, it doesn't matter. I don't care. Really. Do what you think is best."

He recognized my need to justify myself. Such a logical kid. So above all this—so not emotionally handcuffed to the divorce. *How does he cope as well as he does? Does he? Maybe I'm not recognizing some deeper problem.*

I woke the next day in a bitter mood. The whole camera thing brought up bad divorce memories I never wanted to revisit. A day at the beach might brighten my mood, but outside the sky was darkening, and it was only 9 AM.

I had planned to take the backroads to the beach at Ogunquit, wander the shore, catch some sun, and have a lobster lunch somewhere but, some days you should stay in bed. We got off to a late start; it was pouring rain most of the way and the roads were slow, wet, crowded, and narrow. It was a Saturday, which was part of the problem. The locals were heading for the beach towns, too. I finally found the road to Ogunquit, but it looked like a parking lot. The line of traffic on the one-lane road was backed up for at least a mile and if you missed the turn, you would have to turn around and wait in the line again, going the other way, which of course, I did. It was so crowded I decided to forget Ogunquit. Instead, I turned around and looked for a less populated place for lunch that had a view of the rugged North Atlantic coastline. But the more I drove, the worse traffic got.

Besides the traffic, I was angry at myself and arguing with Tom in my head. I didn't want to relive those days. Silently, I stopped the car, put the camera back in the box, and shoved it into a tight crevice behind my seat, knowing I would have nothing more to do or say about Tom, the camera, or his plan.

After a lunch stop at a small cafe, I got on the Interstate, and we rolled on through Maine without a beach stop or a lobster lunch. We headed for Boston.

Cirque de Soleil's *Alegria* was playing on the CD. I loved the music and the message—the passing of power—the transformation of generations. While I couldn't transform a generation, I could do something transformative that day—I could leave all my divorce baggage in Maine. I imagined some dirty, scruffy little island off the farthest point of Maine. Nothing lived there. It was just marsh and ice, and that's where I dumped all the Tom baggage for the rest of the trip.

Above: Ready to go with our Toshiba laptop, Motorola flip phone and fully packed Chevrolet Blazer. Photo taken by the Los Gatos newspaper. Yes, his middle finger is out, and I think he knew it. Below: Camping, marshmallows, and our evening toast. Photo taken with camera timer.

Always searching for lizards.

Road Noise

Above: At the antler arch in Jackson Wyoming ready for the shootout
Below: Trying to cool off in a Grant Park fountain in Chicago.

DJ Lynn

Above: On one of our Moab Utah, Arches hikes
Below: Grand Canyon rim after the Blue Angel trail hike

Above: Old North Cemetery Concord, New Hampshire
Below: Relaxing in Boston

Boston Moon

Boston, Massachusetts

The Friendly Crossways Hostel was a rambling and old, converted farmhouse in Harvard just outside of Boston. It had been remodeled for efficiency and bed space, not style. It was nearly full due to the annual meeting of the Children of the Bruderhof or the former members of the Hutterian Brethren, a group of Christians that trace origins to sixteenth century Europe.

A conversation with a small group of women standing around the lobby that morning provided a bit of insight since I had never heard of the group. The group bears some resemblance to the Amish in clothing, ideologies, and the communal way of living. They reject state churches, practice adult baptism, are strict pacifists, and adhere to common ownership of property. The faith demands public confession, repentance of sin, and ostracism of member sinners back to the world.

At the time we were there, the Bruderhof organization was going through a substantial upheaval that included a rebellion of former members. The overriding issue was the complete and permanent separation of families if one member becomes an enemy of the faith through some transgression and gets tossed out. There was a pending lawsuit, threats of violence, and the usual backlash from church members against those speaking out. Sounded to me like all organized religion—they demand control over and destruction of the self. Of course, that is the most efficient way of keeping believers in line—religious or political.

Steve was starting school soon, so the next couple of weeks would be a long educational field trip. We would start with Concord's many historical sites and then into Boston for the Boston Tea Party Museum, The Old North Church, Quincy Market, and the Mayflower II (a replica of the original).

We also saw the Computer Museum, a stop of particular interest to Steve, who was already tech-savvy, having grown up with two tech parents and a variety of technology equipment.

On Sunday, we listened to jazz at Quincy Market and stopped to watch a variety of performers—everything from street drummers to guys on stilts and female contortionists. Steve asked for trinket money and ran off down the mall. He came back with a large, long-legged, long-armed stuffed monkey with sunglasses and a permanent laughing smile. It was attached to a long stick. If you carried it right, it jiggled and twisted like it was alive and walking with you, something akin to that invisible dog we saw in Toronto. Steve teased a few people with it, and their smiles and laughter kept him going. He took particular interest in teasing the girls—of any age.

In the Friendly Crossways dorm room that evening, I met Kathy, a late-thirties Los Angeles cinematographer in Boston to meet with an eye specialist for a tumor in her right eye. She was scared, looking for answers and re-examining her LA lifestyle. We shared some common interests, mostly escapist ideas like moving to Panama or crossing the Outback on a camel. A more practical idea, we thought, would be to visit Henry David Thoreau's Walden Pond the next morning.

Kathy would join us there. We would start with a quiet, meditative morning at Walden Pond and then have lunch before going our separate ways. While there, maybe we could capture a moment of Thoreau in a short reading of his book, *Walden*.

> "*I wanted... to drive life into a corner, and reduce it to its lowest terms, and, if it proved to be mean, why then to get the whole and genuine meanness of it, and publish its meanness to the world; or if it were sublime, to know it by experience...*"

Months before the trip, I had pictured certain things—the way things were likely to be—setting my expectations for peace of mind and attempting to determine what Steve, an energetic pre-teen, would tolerate, and for how long. There would be things that I couldn't do with a child on board. But some things I knew I had to do for myself, and Steve would just have to deal with those for an hour or so and I would do the same for his unappealing activities, like watching him circle around another go-kart track.

So, I saw myself sitting beside Walden Pond with my battered copy of *Walden* reading a few short passages to Steve that I thought would hold his attention for a moment or two before he scrambled back to the shore digging his hands into the mud and water looking for frogs. I had pictured Walden Pond as a small and semi-deserted, nearly dried-up pool of water sitting in relative obscurity in the burbs of Boston. I thought there would be a plaque to Thoreau discriminately placed, a dozen students prone on the grass reading, a handful of older former-hippy-ish tourists, mostly without kids, and a half-dozen thirty-somethings in running shoes and spandex drinking bottled water and whispering intently to each other something of extreme importance. That was not the reality. As so many things go—there went my illusions of Walden Pond.

Parking near the pond was full, and the city had closed the pond that day to more auto traffic. But you could walk in—and they did. Various sizes and ages of pond goers, in bright floral swimsuits and plastic flip-flops, two or three little kids in tow trekked a quarter of a mile from the school parking lot down the hill carrying neon inflatables, lawn chairs, and insulated coolers.

I suppose, had I gotten past the pond swimmers and picnic spreads and kids throwing Frisbees, I would have found that quiet spot, at least for a moment or two, but the crowds discouraged me, and Steve didn't care. Instead, Kathy and I converged on a coffee shop a few miles away where we drank lattes and said our goodbyes.

Steve and I headed for Plymouth, The Rock, the Mayflower, the museum, and a cute bed-and-breakfast place only blocks from the marina, The Bunk and Bagel. For the first time in a few weeks, we took the bikes to sightsee. I sat on the shore and soaked up the afternoon. Steve fished out what he thought was a shark jawbone in the water and then hunted down horseshoe crabs and gently attended to other assorted seashore life.

The Plimoth Plantation was a Boston highlight. It was an expensive but worthwhile look into life in the 1600s. Actors stayed in the character of those English settlers that arrived on the Mayflower. There was a group of Native Americans representing the tribes of the Wampanoag people on the Plantation, separated, as they would have been, from the colony. You could ask the actors anything about their life up until 1620, and they knew their history. If you asked them questions post-1620, they stayed in character and played dumb.

Steve took a particular interest in the Wampanoag and their pottery making. The pots they made at the Plantation were for their own use on the reservation and there were not enough supplies for visitors to join in, but somehow Steve charmed them, as he does, and they asked him to sit and make a pot with them. For over an hour, I watched him from a bench not far away as he sat with them and learned the coil method of pottery making. They included him in the next demonstration to Plantation visitors.

A Boston moon appeared as the sun was setting. Steve and I sat on an outdoor deck at the Lobster Hut overlooking the Plymouth Marina. I finally got my lobster and a front-row seat to a boat show. The Hut was a local spot to watch tourists put in their boats. A few people around us on the deck pointed to the ramp.

Steve picked up on their conversations and said, "Mom, look at the dock ramp."

An SUV was backing a Stingray—about twenty feet long, down the ramp. Grandma and grandpa had gotten out of the car and were standing on the dock. The wife was at the wheel of the SUV while the husband got into the boat. With the boat partially in the water, he started up the engine and tried to back it off the trailer. I know little about boats, but the boat was not moving, and it looked like the bow strap had not been removed. He punched the engine hard astern. The boat began to pull the trailer, with SUV still attached, backward toward the water. The wife was now standing up on the brakes, but the car was still inching down the ramp. Finally, the husband seemed to clue in, slowing the boat engine while almost simultaneously jumping to the bow strap, getting it off just as the wife and the SUV were about to go down with the boat. Several people at the Lobster Hut were now clapping and laughing. The show was over—at least for tonight.

Obsessions & Opposites

New York City

It was 1981, three years into our marriage, six years before our divorce, two years before Steve was born, and the year John Holmes the porn star claimed he did 14,000 women with his fifteen-inch *johnson*. I was in New York City with Tom on a two-day stopover on our way to London on business. It was my first time in the city, actually my first time in any big city as a tourist. Tom was not interested in the MoMA or The Met, but he liked to shop at Saks, eat at Le Cirque, or whatever restaurant was trending at the moment, and when I wasn't along on his business trips, he would explore the nightlife. That night, he said he wanted to surprise me. We had a fancy dinner somewhere I can't remember, a Caymus Cabernet, which turned out to be the highlight of the evening, and then—his surprise. He said it was a dance club, and we both loved to dance.

A doorman opened a dark, heavy door for us as if we were expected. It didn't occur to me at the time, but later I questioned that in my head. *Did the doorman know my husband?* Outside there were a few couples and five or six men standing alone smoking. A quiet sign said it was Plato's Retreat. I had only vaguely heard of the New York swingers' club, and although I was no prude, it was not something I would have agreed to had I known where we were going.

Suddenly, I saw naked people—suburbanite women with wide hips and flopping breasts, fat men with pool-wet comb-overs, and twenty-something women with teased blonde hair and red lipstick, which, by some miracle, clung to their lips despite the humidity. Several couples were in a large waist-deep pool and surprisingly bright lighting provided a clear view of their mid-life pale and paunchy bodies.

Although there was no alcohol being served and no bar that I could see, it was obvious other substances were being consumed, most likely Quaaludes or cocaine. I was not interested in drugs, but without a few cocktails, that evening was going nowhere for me.

We wandered around through semi-private rooms—some with equipment of sorts—odd-shaped chairs, swings, poles, and a large room with floor mats and pillows everywhere, and about forty steamy bodies flopping around like fish out of water. I admit I had a few moments of curiosity, but there was a yuck factor I couldn't get past. That, and recent rumors of a new sexually transmitted disease, which was almost always fatal. They were calling it AIDS. The 1970s free love swinger's era was about to come to an abrupt end.

That evening opened a window into our marriage I hadn't seen before. I would have preferred a reading of Keats in the park and an inexpensive bottle of wine followed by sensual sex in our hotel room, but he wanted fancy food and swinger's erotica. That variety might have been okay had there been both in our marriage—a balance, but the faults in our marital compatibility became chasms that weekend in New York City.

. . .

At the hotel, I pocketed $60 and handed Steve my credit card and a slim wad of cash I had folded into a cloth wallet designed to strap around his leg.

"We need to be a little more careful here. All the crowds, you know. It's stuff that can happen in big cities. No big deal, just a precaution," I said casually.

I didn't want to cause him concern. He was a cautious kid and might worry. But he wasn't worried. His face had a perceptible smile. He was proud to be the designated money holder.

"What are we doing today, Meat?"

"There's so much to do here, so today I'm thinking the MoMA, which is the Museum of Modern art, then we'll walk over to Times Square and then try to find the Majestic Theater and see if we can get tickets to *Phantom of the Opera*. Tomorrow we'll go to the Central Park Zoo and take a run around the park. Then the next day take a drive out to Long Island and then to the Liberty Science Center. What do you think?"

"Is there a beach somewhere? And what is phantom and the opera? Is that a movie?"

"We'll stop at a beach out on Long Island. And *Phantom of the Opera* is a musical that is the most popular musical ever. It's been playing at that theater for ten years or so. I think you'll like it, but it's not like anything you've ever seen. I saw it in San Francisco with your dad."

"Is it like *Nutcracker*?"

"Well, it's a musical but much better than *The Nutcracker* we saw in San Jose."

I wasn't sure Steve would understand contemporary art. I wasn't sure I understood, but like all art it's about individual interpretation; what is contemporary and what is art? I thought it would be good to expose Steve to contemporary art because I didn't think he knew what it was and, he was already becoming a nerdy science guy, and I thought he could use some artistic mind expansion. In contemporary art everything is up for grabs, anything can be art; any subject, any idea, any medium—it's just about how we view the world, how we question it, and how we relate to it. He was already doing that, so I thought he should see that other people were too. He may not understand it. Who does? But it was part of my mom-goal to expose him to ideas and keep his mind open.

We both had a particular interest in a video installation called *HardCell*, an assemblage that invoked visions of technology gone wrong. Stenciled black letters on a broken wood crate identified the object as having belonged to the HardCell Corporation. Spilling out were abandoned computer monitors and parts all linked by a nerve-like maze of wires and tubing. It twitched and groaned. Computer messages and code streamed across the monitors as if life-forms were still communicating random thoughts. Cyborgs still at work. A message on the screen scrolled across, *data indicates viral presence but no antibodies.*

We were both intrigued and kept returning to the exhibit for further examination. Steve studied it intently, but only said, "This is art? This is cool."

The rest of the afternoon we walked all over midtown and Times Square and although tempted a few times, I didn't go into any shops except to ask directions to the Majestic Theater. I thought it wouldn't hurt to ask if there were any tickets to *Phantom of the Opera* in the next two days, and we got lucky. There were two seats left for the 8 PM performance the next night.

I wasn't sure how much Steve would understand from the show, but afterwards he said he really liked it and was concerned about the Phantom.

"Mom, was that story based on real-life? Was there really a man that was deformed and what happened to him?"

"I believe it's all fiction, although most stories have elements of truth. I read somewhere that a chandelier fell through the roof of a Paris opera house, and that a deformed man once lived beneath that same opera house. But I doubt if that's true."

Why do we find this love triangle, the theme of so many books, movies, and plays, so moving in *Phantom of the Opera*?

For me, it would not have been the same without the music. You can feel your temperature rise and your heart quicken when you hear *Music of the Night* or *Point of no Return*.

There is also an archetypical agelessness—this guided journey into the depths of man's despair (I think of Dante's inferno) and the redeeming power of love (perhaps like Persephone and Pluto or Beauty and the Beast). And then there is the symbolism—the masquerade scene, and social hypocrisy—a grand Paris opera house contrasted with a dark underground cave isolated by water. Masks to hide our inner dark desires but revealed in the Phantom's sensuality and Christine's euphoria when she's around him. We feel rage as we struggle for love and acceptance and violence when power is evasive. A kiss of understanding and tears of compassion. In the end, the Phantom's desires are undone and raw. He won't get what he wants but can finally accept the truth and depth of his love that goes beyond his desires. His awakening. He is the manifestation of our virtues and vices, and we can't help identifying with his suffering. Our connection to the Phantom is our own long journey for love and acceptance that rarely ends as we would like.

From unrealized love and dark desires to animals and science. Next day, the Central Park Zoo.

Sitting in the middle of Manhattan, the Central Park Zoo is small, but we didn't care. We love all zoos. It didn't take long to realize that the polar bear named Gus had a lot of people around his enclosure. Steve pushed up toward the glass to see what was going on. A thirty-something man with tiny twins was standing back from the crowd with his double stroller, watching two other small children in front of the enclosure. The babies were sleeping peacefully as the man reached into the stroller and pulled the blanket off one of them.

I moved a little closer to him to see the babies, "Twins, how sweet! They look new!"

He smiled, "Two months and it was a surprise. We didn't know there were two until a month before. I have four kids now, all under five, and I'm a little freaked out."

"Oh my, I hope you have some help."

"Grandma's there right now with my wife at home. I'm trying to give them a little break. I bring the kids here a lot. Gives them something to do, and it seems to calm them down for the evening."

"What's going on with the polar bear? Is it feeding time?"

"No, there's a lot of controversy about this bear right now. They think he's depressed or has polar bear OCD or something. He obsessively swims in the same pattern all day. They called in some experts and gave him some toys and more stimulation, and I guess it has helped a little, but he's still not right."

"Oh, that's so sad. What are they going to do?"

"Well, they've tried the stimulation, but I think they're giving him drugs too, like Prozac. Not much they can do, I suppose. Can't let him go. They're going to expand his habitat and add more activities and playthings. I heard they're going to make him hunt for food somehow; see if that helps. But it's not just Gus, the experts are realizing this is going on at a lot of zoos. Animals don't want to be caged. Can't really blame them."

Steve appeared, "Hey Mom, somebody over there said that polar bear is crazy. I think he looks sad."

I said *good luck* to the man with the babies and Steve and I moved on.

"Yeah, I think you're right. He's sad and depressed not crazy. Are you ready to leave the zoo and take a run around the park? And tonight, for dinner, there's a place called the Jekyll and Hyde Club, some sort of spooky restaurant. You want to go there?"

"A spooky restaurant?"

"I think they have creepy sounding food names and some guy walking around in a vampire costume making creepy sounds. What do you think?"

"Can I make creepy sounds too?"

"Actually, you probably can."

Next day, a quick drive to a beach on Long Island and then a visit to the Liberty Science Center, but it was not quick. Just getting to Jones Beach took a couple of hours and traffic was heavy, but we had lunch, splashed around in the ocean, and sunk our toes in the sugary sand.

The Liberty Science Center in New Jersey took us through

the brain in 3D and let us experience classic Newtonian physics like the laws of motion in a Bernoulli blower, the waves and resonance of a sonic tube, and the interference of light waves in soap bubbles. I let Steve wander around on his own; it would have been impossible to keep up with him.

I stood hypnotized, observing the arms of the impossible triangle. It looked as if they touch. The brain wants to make sense of it and make it possible, but our eyes deceive us of the reality.

The Phantom's doom was still on my mind. *We don't always get what we want. We don't always see what's real.*

Road Noise

Can't Stop Dancing

Hershey, Pennsylvania to
Hagerstown, Maryland

We stopped at a small cafe in Hershey at around 10 AM. We were on the way to Washington, DC for a three-day education-focused stay, but Steve saw signs about a Hershey tour and an amusement park and about ten other Hershey related activities and was loudly demanding some theme park related entertainment. I was in no mood for a chocolate-themed amusement park and reminded him we would be in Orlando in a week. He wasn't happy and for the first time on the trip, we argued.

I was tired and edgy from white-knuckle driving on Interstates, fighting congested big city downtown traffic, honking for no apparent reason, or maybe for any reason at all, pedestrians crossing against lights, people on bikes, narrow tunnels, and one-way streets that took me hours, or maybe it was minutes, out of my way. It would be days before I would get a reprieve from my driving anxiety at a hostel on the Blue Ridge Parkway. I needed some space to breathe and did not want to rub up next to hundreds of people waiting in line for roller coasters and cotton candy, let alone spend a bunch of money for just another amusement park—they all looked the same to me.

The Hershey name was everywhere, street names, parks, gardens, golf courses, fire stations, hotels, restaurants, housing communities, and an entertainment park and stadium. Hershey didn't just build a chocolate factory he built an entire town.

"I just can't go to an amusement park today. Can you please pick something else that's less crazy and doesn't take all day? I'm tired of all the driving. I need a break."

"You can take a break at the amusement park; you don't have to go on any of the rides."

I knew his tone, and he would not leave this one alone. How much was I willing to fight for some peace and quiet?

"I can't leave you alone to wander some giant amusement park on your own. It's unsafe."

His tone was growing more frustrated, "Mom, I'm nearly twelve and almost as tall as you. Give it a rest."

I sighed and felt like I might cry. My voice got tired and quiet. "I'm not going on any rides. I'm going to sit at some cafe, and you have to come and check in with me every thirty minutes. And don't talk to any weirdos—I think that would be any adult without kids. And don't leave the park."

"Seriously, Mom? Don't talk to weirdos and don't leave the park? What will I do then?"

After buying a book at the gift shop at Hershey Park on the history of Hershey, I found a small cafe, and against my normal dietary habits, which I'd already blown by eating at a fast-food place earlier, I bought a chocolate soda and sat at an outdoor umbrella-covered table. Over the next three hours, Steve checked in with me three times, trying desperately to make me happy again. He'd met a father with two boys around his age and had spent much of his time with them on the roller coasters and at the arcade. I was grateful for his companions, and out of guilt gave him more money.

As I sat people watching and occasionally glancing at the book, I remembered we were only miles from Harrisburg, which is where my parents were married. My family on both sides were from Pennsylvania Dutch country. Although I didn't know exactly what that meant, I knew Hershey was one of the towns.

There I was, basically against my will, in the very place where my parents and grandparents lived; the people I grew up with but never really knew. Perhaps it was their nature, or maybe just the times. Children weren't participants in a family so much as they were permanent foreign guests—to be taught the language, the culture, the religion, and shaped to be the next identical generation—little clones of parents-past.

I let my mind wander to vague memories of my parents and grandparents as they were in their younger years. I thought it odd how little I knew of them, but they never talked much about their past, or really anything at all that didn't involve the church. What I remembered were fragments I had pieced together over the years, mostly from a few stories from my father and a handful of photos salvaged from a flood that consumed the basement of the church where we lived.

My father grew up on a dairy farm near Pottsville. His parents disowned him when he was sixteen after he started preaching for a group calling themselves the Bible Students. He moved to Pittsburgh, got a job throwing papers, and continued his preaching to anyone who would listen. Although he tried, neither his parents nor any of his three brothers, ever reconciled with him. My brother and I never met or knew our grandparents, aunts, uncles, or cousins on his side of the family.

My mother and her family were from Pittsburgh and were all part of the Bible Student movement under the millennialist teachings of Charles Taze Russell that claimed Christ would reign for a literal 1,000 peaceful years before calling the final judgment on the world. The movement was associated with the formation of the Watchtower Bible and Tract Society and the later formation of the Jehovah's Witnesses in 1931 whose beliefs by then had diverged considerably from Russell's teachings.

In late July 1931, at age eighteen, my father took a bus to Columbus, Ohio to attend an international convention where they officially adopted the name Jehovah's Witnesses. It was there he met Victoria, a seventeen-year-old girl from Dayton. Early in 1932 they married, moved to Youngstown, and ten months later had a baby girl. Three years later the girl would drown in a local lake and before the year was out, Victoria would be killed by a car speeding down an alley while my father walked at her side.

At age twenty-three and deeply in mourning, he became a pioneer for the Watchtower Society, and not long later, a sought-after traveling preacher. A year later he met my mother while delivering a sermon at a small congregation in Bradford, Pennsylvania.

Within a year, they got married, attended a Bible school called Gilead, and became missionaries, first in the rural south, and then accepted an assignment in the Philippines. There were lots of pictures of them and the congregation they helped set up in and around Manila. They didn't plan to return to the US, except my mother accidentally got pregnant. Missionaries were not allowed to have children, so the Watchtower Society sent them home to the US, specifically to form a congregation near the growing edge of Denver.

I didn't know I was an unwanted child until I was in my thirties and did some background reading about religion. I don't recall being upset about it. My parents were good people and meant well, and my father became a well-loved speaker and pastor, or congregation servant, as they were called.

My grandparents on my mother's side were also part of the Russell Bible Student movement, but what I remember most about them had nothing to do with their religion. They were the perfect couple. I knew that, even as a child. They kissed and hugged each other all the time, and I never remember a raised voice, or an unkind word being spoken about anyone.

Memories of my grandparent's house in Pittsburgh are as hazy as the lacy curtains that hung in the dining room, the only room I remember well. The room was graced with grand wood cabinets full of patterned china and a table with curled-up claw feet that seemed to tower over me. Random images in my head were of wooden people-shaped clothespins and a clothesline outside that spun in the wind like a top, finely crocheted tablecloths, and a kitchen that always had a pie on the counter and a stew on the stove. The smell of the house made you want to eat. Concord grapes grew wild in the backyard, and I ate them until I was sick, and Grandma Mary gave me homemade ginger ale.

They had stuff. Lots of stuff—the kind that accumulates after many years of marriage to the same person and a lifetime of living in the same place. There were hutches full of old plates, silver, and embroidered napkins. In the basement, there were hooks holding keys to locks I can't imagine existed and shelves with rows of boxes and bins and items standing alone. The edges of the shelves were neatly labeled with the items that were sitting on it. There were old mattresses Grandpa Harry would put out for us to jump on and old clothes in dark wood chests that I dressed my little brother in, and a small, windowed attic that looked like a big dollhouse that, even as a five-year-old, I had to stoop to get into.

Harry was one of those perpetual smilers. His purple cheeks looked like big plums, and his tousled and wavy salt and pepper gray hair was always hanging over one eye. I thought he must have been a good-looking young man. He was quick with the jokes, always squeaky clean, and teased us with magic tricks. He was never without his Magic Marker (invented only a few years earlier) which he kept in his pants pocket with a neatly folded white handkerchief.

He had marked the cots in the basement with the words *head* and *foot* because, I guessed, people might object to sleeping at the wrong end of a cot. He wasn't far from one of his many special flashlights. There were several in the house, strategically placed. They were about fourteen inches long, heavy, and with a wide head which Harry had wrapped with about a thousand rounds of duct tape (also recently invented). The head of the flashlight was as big as a club, and I guess that's what he planned to use it for if it ever came down to it. Harry and Mary were pacifists, and the duct tape club would be the only weapon in the house, except maybe for Harry's preaching.

In the afternoons, Grandpa Harry would always take us for ice cream in his big blue Oldsmobile. It had a baseball size compass mounted in the center of the dash. The floating needle in the big black ball wiggled hypnotically as I stared at it with my chin resting on the back of the front seat. My brother kneeled on the front seat so he could see out of the wide front window. Sometimes, on a quiet backstreet, grandpa would let us steer the car for a few seconds. It seemed like centuries ago. In a way, it was. Harry and Mary are long gone now, and so was their way of life—the days when people stayed married and stayed put.

I admire those that stay put, but I also think they miss a lot of life. A good friend once joked that I might consider therapy because I moved so much—jobs, cities, husbands. I can't stop dancing. I counted the moves a while back. There were twenty-three in thirty-five years and numbers like that belong in the ranks of thieves and elephant migrations. I agree that I may have some tendencies, but I am still quite a few quirks away from a disorder. The result may not have been as I hoped (often it was destructive and a waste of money) but there were always good reasons at the time. My life has never been boring. It occurred to me that I have always been running and dancing away from the childhood I had and toward the imaginary one I wished for.

Steve made a final appearance at my table and said we could go now. His cheeks were pink, his shirt was wet and had something spilled down the front. He looked tired. After three and a half hours, a lot of sugar and spinning rides, he was finally ready to leave.

"Did you get some rest, Mom? I tried not to bug you."

He gave me a hug and his sweet voice made me wish I'd gone on at least a few rides with him.

What was the matter with me? I should have been nicer. I should have been there with him.

"Yes, thank you, and you didn't bug me. Sorry I was cranky earlier. Did you have fun?"

"I did. I hung around with those guys most of the time. They were cool, and they liked the roller coasters just like me."

I kissed his head. "Great. I'm glad you had a good time. Do you want to get on the road now and maybe get some real food somewhere? What do you feel like?"

Two hours later I pulled into a Hagerstown, Maryland cheap motel. It didn't look bad on the outside, and I ignored my recent rule to see the room first. A heavy musty odor hit me in the face as I opened the door to the room. It had been brewing for days in the ninety-plus heat, and I could feel my nasal passages swell. The carpet, originally two-inch green shag, was now a dull greenish-brown stiff mat. I would keep my shoes on. The beds and bath passed my usual inspection, although we would still sleep in the sleeping bags on the bed. Except for the acquisition of more pint-sized towels, the room would do for a night. It was hot, humid, and it would soon rain—thankfully because the air conditioner didn't work. Oblivious to my mumbling complaints, Steve watched cartoons while cicadas hummed unconcerned in nearby trees.

Next stop: Washington, DC, where we would stay put for the longest as any on this trip—three entire days.

Road Noise

Great Chain of Bugs

Washington, DC

Little towns and big cities were tumbling past one after the other now. Each seemed only miles from the last, yet distinct. Old brick colonials and little pristine white churches sat quietly in one town and a few miles further, contemporary wood framed townhomes circled an urban shopping mall. I noticed few had fences, but this is not a testament to less crime but a social community that will risk some measure of security as an invitation to friendly neighbors. That's nice. I come from California, where buttoned up and sealed off from potentially incompatible neighbors is the preferred state of being.

There is no mistaking DC. It is skillfully structured to provide an immediate feeling of a place in control. We know who they were and the symbolism. Masons. Pagan. Occult. Druids. Aliens. Whatever. Pagan and occult symbolism pervade organized religion, our financial systems, and our holidays. I don't mind, but I wonder why those concerned about their religious rituals don't.

∞

Road Noise

The Howard Johnson in Alexandria, Virginia, being south of DC, provided a lower room rate and nice accommodations. Except for the night manager, the staff was helpful and pleasant, particularly the maintenance man who came up three times to fix the phone and the television and continued to be pleasant despite my tart attitude on the third call.

The plan for the next day was to do as many museums on the mall as we could squeeze in on a hot and humid day without passing out. We would start with the American and Natural History and then do the Hirshhorn, the Smithsonian Gardens, African Art, and the Freer. They say it's only a mile between them all, but with all the walking within the museums—it must be a twenty-mile day. The next day, if I could still walk, we would do the various memorials and monuments.

We stayed quite a while at the Insect Zoo of the Natural History Museum. Bugs have been a favorite of Steve's since he was a toddler. At age three, at a bookstore in Palo Alto, he found a book full of color photos and explanations of hundreds of bugs, *The Audubon Society Book of Insects*. It was nearly as big as he was. For the next several years, it was his book of choice for the bedtime power-down.

In the great chain of being, insects are far down the links. Yet bugs have innate knowledge about the world. Several years ago, outside the building of a company where I worked, I sat on the concrete ledge of a fountain. I attempted to subvert my stress and distaste for the company by fake smoking while watching a large group of ants pass the fountain in an organized liner path to a wide expanse of grass a half-dozen feet away. They were all carrying something. One ant had become disoriented or something. Perhaps I had stepped lightly on him? He looked fine, except he was moving in circles and weaving in and out of the ant traffic. Most ants just passed him by. Some slowed and gave him a once-over with their antennae and moved on. Then, a minute later two ants came from the direction of the grass. Home? It seemed they had been passed a message by incoming ants because they came directly to him. They did a little antennae thing all over him and then picked him up together and carried him toward the grass. Was he ill, dying, old? Were they saving him or taking him back home for lunch?

Why the ant event stuck in my memory is curious. These tiny creatures have a system, a plan, a set of knowledge that arrived with them. It was inherent when they were born. Was it already coded into their minuscule brain? Or did it exist without them in a field of vibration exactly right for the frequency of the Carpenter Ant?

My thinking about the Akashic field theory or some sort of universal source of knowledge, while staring at the giant dino-whale hanging from the ceiling of the Natural History Museum, was shattered by the sound of my name being called.

"Hey, Mom. There's a place to eat and a gift shop downstairs. I asked that guy."

He pointed to a tall forty-something man in an old Army

jacket and jeans standing alone near the stairwell. I frowned to myself.

"I don't think he works here. You know, you need to be careful about who you talk to. You know, strangers and all that."

"Mom, everybody is a stranger. Hello Pinky. We don't live here."

"Yes, Brain, but you know what I mean. Ask people in uniforms or that have badges or something."

Badges or uniforms? I think I noticed his eyebrow raise. He was so much smarter than that. I sighed. What do I say? Am I profiling all guys in Army jackets standing alone near stairwells in national museums? I brushed away the worries that always dog me with him, as a flash of the memory of Adam Walsh crossed my mind.

"Good idea. Let's eat. Lead me to it."

He led me down the stairs right past the man in the Army jacket. We caught each other's eyes, and I couldn't tell if he looked like a perv or not.

Stars of Galax

Urbanna to Galax, Virginia

Boston, New York, DC—I was spinning with history, science, nature, crowds, and white knuckle driving through honking horns and jaywalkers. The chaos had consumed me. My introversion was showing. I needed to retreat. I would soon get that chance. We were on our way into the soft heart of Virginia where we would meet two of the most interesting people on this trip.

It seemed like the only roads in coastal Virginia were backroads. Little idyllic treasures. Old. Rustic. So green. I got lost a few times. I don't recall many road signs. The Sangraal-by-the-Sea hostel was actually by-the-river Rappahannock near Urbanna on the Chesapeake Bay.

The hostel was nearly hidden and sat on a wooded multi-acre property. The main house was a colonial wood-frame. The hostel was separated from the house and was a large open dorm-style room. The property was surrounded by a lush overgrowth that reminded me of England—creepers and vines with tiny flowers, wide dense trees, leaves inches deep on cracked stone paths and a short walk to an old pier on the river.

As the only guests, we had the entire place to ourselves. It had a kitchen, large table, and a piano. Above and around the sides were two lofts, each with several single mattresses on the floor. The air conditioning barely cooled the lower area, and the lofts were stifling, somewhat dirty, and housed a variety of cobwebs. Earlier, I had seen a couple of black widow spiders and decided I was sleeping with the lights on, hoping that would keep the spiders away.

Sherry, the manager, was a young girl from London barely in her twenties. Steve and Sherry hit it off immediately, and I heard laughter, basketball, and the piano until after dark. I was grateful for a few hours alone and immersed myself in a book.

My spirits lifted with the sunrise. I made breakfast, and then we took the trail to the sea. Steve immediately rushed out to the end of the pier. I sat at on the dock, trying to avoid sitting on the bolts in the planks that were already fire hot. Steve plopped down on his stomach, head over the end, trying to fish something out of the water.

A man with a young boy about age three nodded at me as he walked out to a small blue boat that rocked gently in the water. The man looked to be about forty-five with short gray hair, sturdy legs, and a round, clean-shaven, uncomplicated face. We exchanged greetings as they prepared to motor out. A few minutes later, a dark-haired woman walked out toward us. She asked if I had seen the man and boy.

"They left about five minutes ago," I said.

"Oh. I decided I'd go. I was hoping to catch them."

Her voice was sad, and she spoke quietly, almost in a whisper.

"I had a headache earlier. Still do, but I wanted to go with them."

She was extremely attractive, with wavy brown hair and deep dimples. Her body was round but shapely; her red top tucked neatly into khaki shorts.

"I guess I'll wait a bit. Do you mind?"

"Of course not," I said. "Sit."

We exchanged names and sparse details of our reasons to be sitting on the pier that day. She expressed curiosity about our trip, but with a tone of concern. Wasn't I worried about being alone on such a long journey? It's so brave of you!

I had never once worried about being alone and *brave* was not a word I associated with our trip, although I heard it said several times. What people meant was that they thought it was brave that I would do this trip without a man along. Why? Because he could protect me, change a tire, drive smoother, navigate a map better?

"Well, I'm not alone, my son is with me."

It was the halfway point of this adventure with Steve. I wondered what I would take back that will make this trip worthwhile. No grand revelations had descended on me yet, and I was waiting for them—I wanted a bolt of enlightenment to strike me. Will I have learned something about myself? Will I provide the ultimate experience for Steve solidifying myself forever as the ultimate cool mom? If so, will the sacrifice forever overwrite my actual maternal inadequacies? *Oh, what a sad thing I was, all these questions, all this complaining. Where was my patience? My introspection? Was I trying hard enough to discover something? Or was I just driving.*

After a few sightseeing stops and time visiting Colonial Williamsburg about thirty minutes south, we were on our way toward the Blue Ridge Parkway and a hostel in Galax, Virginia, near the North Carolina border.

. . .

It was the week and year of the 60th Annual Old Fiddlers' Convention in Galax, Virginia. If you could play a bluegrass fiddle, dulcimer, autoharp, dobro, or mandolin, you were there playing the classics like *Foggy Mountain Special* or *Leather Britches.*

Nancy Sluys won first place on her clawhammer banjo. The New Ballard's Branch Bog Trotters, a local Galax group, won best Old Time Band and All-Around Best Performer was Nate Leath. He was eleven years old. Same age as Steve.

Galax was in the heart of the Blue Ridge Mountains, about three hours northwest of Raleigh. We were headed toward the Virginia Blue Ridge Hostel. Alex and Lois Koji built a second story on their home in 1988 specifically to take in the world travelers who came to hike or cycle the Blue Ridge Parkway or Cumberland Knob or attend one of the many bluegrass music festivals in the area. They had the hospitality and warm hearts for such an undertaking.

Alex and Lois greeted us and showed us around. Steve immediately took to their three dogs, Nitro, Minnie Mouse, and Oatmeal, who were thrilled to have someone tirelessly throw sticks for them to chase. Alex was retired having been in aviation manufacturing for decades. Lois was a Chicago educated musician and craftswoman—a woman of many talents and a favorite pastime was scherenschnitte, or paper cutting she learned from her father.

Later in the evening, Lois showed us the main house. I could have explored it for days. On every surface, there were baskets and bins of colored craft paper, ribbons, wooden spools, and magazines. Lois was gifted at recycling just about everything into something else. She showed Steve how to make a paper necklace and Moravian stars. She had hundreds of the stars around the house and crafted a special one for each departing guest as good luck on their journey.

Most impressive was the music room full of old and unusual instruments, and Lois played all of them. There were several types of fiddles and mandolins, dulcimers, autoharps, and banjos. She referred to the sound as Old-Time music, which is mostly instrumental and usually led by a fiddle—a string band with a tempo for square dancing. The sound brought back vague memories of the square-dances we went to as a family when I was very small—memories of standing on my father's shoes as he whirled me around and around on a sawdust-covered floor to the rhythms of the *Licorice Stick Polka*.

An element of Old-Time music is the banjo played claw-hammer style, where the fingers strike the strings in a down picking motion. According to Lois, this picking style contrasts with the traditional, which consists of an up-picking motion by the fingers and down-picking motion by the thumb. She demonstrated and Steve and I tried. Our attempts sounded like a couple of cats being poked.

There was only one man staying at the hostel. He was perhaps a little older than me—tall, late forties, I guessed. It's often hard to tell age with men. Brandon, who had an aristocratic British accent, preferred to be called Bryn. He had a rugged, tanned but youthful face and a bit of silver in his dark hair.

Steve was obsessed with all the unusual instruments and had gone to the main house to talk to Lois and play with the dogs. I placed our bags onto two of the beds and pulled up an old rocker to sit with a book.

I felt eyes on me. I looked up to see Bryn standing by the window looking at me. He was backlit and I couldn't see his face clearly, only the shape of his slim hiker's body against the light.

"You look so familiar," he said. "Is it possible we know each other?"

I love that opening line, but somehow, he seemed genuine. We exchanged a few comments about our backgrounds, and it didn't seem a possibility that we knew each other, but we agreed there was something familiar we both felt. And then there was an obvious physical attraction.

"Why do you prefer Bryn?"

"Brandon is stuffy, and Bryn is from my Welsh heritage and means *hill*. I love hiking and being out in nature. I've done a lot of travel and the name seemed more fitting. But my father will only call me Brandon."

On that hot August afternoon that rambled smoothly into the night like it was meant to be, Bryn and I shared stories of our lives. With each description of his life, I felt mine sink into the mundane and cliché.

His family home was in East Sussex, England. I immediately imagined a large brick house with a half-acre of grass in front. Bryn had just finished remodeling his own place, an old church near Wadhurst. My mind went blank, I couldn't quite imagine remodeling a church into a house, but I did see lots of big stones, gothic style peeked roofs and flying buttresses.

His father, who used to be a diplomat, started and was now chairman of an investment firm in London working with industries in sub-Saharan Africa, London, and India, but the man's first love is his vineyard. Now I was seeing a grand estate set on wide acres with a stable in the back and Arabian horses in a paddock.

Bryn went to Cambridge for a degree in economics and afterward joined the Royal Air Force.

And me? I got married—twice, got divorced—twice, and had a boring career in marketing...

"Are you with your father's firm now?"

"My older brother is working with him, but it wasn't for me. I went for economics at university because that's what my father wanted. I really wanted to be a naturalist or conservationist—anything but working in a stuffy London high rise with a bunch of suits. So, I became a bush pilot."

I think my mouth fell open, and I had a look of silly astonishment on my face. "A bush pilot? Where?"

"I got a taste of it while in the Air Force in South Africa. Then I read about conservation efforts in Tanzania—the Serengeti and Ngorongoro Crater and felt like I wanted to be part of that somehow. So, I flew into Arusha, bought a Cessna 180, and within a week I was flying safari tourists, conservationists, and filmmakers, mostly around the Serengeti and Kilimanjaro."

Suddenly I started laughing hysterically and then waving my hands saying *No, No,* it's not about you.

"So, you're smart, rich and a bush pilot?" I was still laughing. "That's so iconic that I have no words. I don't mean any offense. I'm incredibly impressed."

Then, I pointed to the book on the coffee table I saw him put down earlier, "And—I see you're reading T. S. Eliot, the *Four Quartets.* Who understands Eliot? Well, except maybe an economist African bush pilot." I was still laughing.

Thank god he started to laugh.

"Well, I never had anyone call me out on all that," he said. "Smart is a matter of opinion and my wealth had nothing to do with me, in fact I'm a negative on that end of the scale. But I really did enjoy being a bush pilot; felt like I was accomplishing something important."

"I'm seriously not laughing at you. I'm sorry if I offended you."

"You didn't offend me. I'm charmed by your honesty and sense of humor."

He produced a broad smile, revealing beautiful white teeth, while a dark curl hung down on his forehead. There was a minute of silence as we held our gaze and watched each other smile. I could feel the heat rising from my chest, so I got up to get a bottle of water.

"You're not flying in Africa anymore?"

"No, I had an accident about a year ago; a minor one really, but I broke both arms and a couple of ribs, but everything healed fine. I just don't feel comfortable flying other people around now and, to be honest, the accident spooked me. That's not a good look for a pilot."

"I'm so sorry. That sounds like a terrible accident, but I understand about not flying as much. Healing bones is easier than healing the mind. What are you going to do now?"

"I decided to come to the US again and do some hiking and decide what I'm doing next. That's why I'm here now. Started at Mount Rainier, working my way east—Tetons,

Grand Canyon, Zion, the Blue Ridge, then part of the Appalachian Trail, and then…not sure."

He smiled again and continued, "You know, I bought some veggies at the market this morning. Can I make you dinner—you and Steve? I'm actually a pretty good cook."

"Of course, you are," I laughed. "I'd love to have dinner with you if you'll explain T. S. Eliot to me. And do you like scotch?"

I reached into my tote and pulled out a small plastic drugstore bag. "Airplane bottles of Ledaig 10. I don't drink much but the small bottles travel well. I don't know how to pronounce it, but it seemed like good scotch because it was more expensive than the other ones."

"I love scotch and it's pronounced *Led-chig* or even *Le-dig* because the *d* and *ch* sounds are almost silent, but it helps to have a guttural Gaelic accent."

"Don't tell me you speak Gaelic too."

He laughed, "No, but I've spent a lot of time in Scotland, and if you pronounce it wrong, they correct you."

I went to the main house to check on Steve. It had been a while since I'd heard from him. He and Lois were still sitting in the dining room folding paper strips into Moravian stars. Lois was clearly taken with Steve and asked if he could have dinner with them because she was going to show him how to play the mandolin afterwards. What a treat for me and him. I was happy to get a few more hours alone with Bryn.

I went back upstairs to the hostel, took a shower, and dug around in my bag to find something more appealing to wear than my shorts, T-shirts, and hiking boots I had been living in for the past two months. I found some clean white shorts and my sleeveless Vermont shirt that had a lower cut neckline and walked back out to the kitchen.

"Steve wants to eat with Lois. They're paper cutting and playing the mandolin."

"He's an interesting young man, and as much as I'd like to get to know him, it will be nice to have a little more time alone with you." He handed me a plate then raised his glass. "Here's to fresh vegetables, quinoa, good scotch, and great company."

Six twin size beds sat around the perimeter of the room. We sat in the middle of the floor on a blanket like a picnic and for the longest time talked about his experiences in the Serengeti and the animals he felt privileged to see. After two scotches, or maybe it was six, we were getting playful and had a pillow fight with the wispy thin pillows until we both fell backwards onto the floor laughing and staring up at the vaulted ceiling.

"Tell me more about you," he said. "Not the divorce and work and kid's stuff. Tell me who you are."

"Well, I can tell you where I am now—who I am trying to be. You know, I don't remember much of T. S. Eliot's work. It often confused me to be honest, but I don't feel stupid because I think he confused a lot of people. Although I don't usually understand his thinking behind the words, I did love his words and I remember these from the Four Quartets."

We shall not cease from exploration
And the end of all our exploring
Will be to arrive where we started
And know the place for the first time.

"I think that sums me up. I'm an explorer, but not of foreign lands. But I'm hoping for that outcome on this journey. I would like to think I could know myself again for the first time, like I could somehow start over with optimistic and more intelligent eyes. But I think the reality of Eliot's words is that it doesn't happen that way."

"That's one of my favorites, but yes, Eliot may have meant those words in a different way. I think it's important to interpret Eliot the way you want to and just lose yourself in the words—make them yours, like you did. But that's the beauty of all poetry and art. You take from it what you need to. What it means to you is what's important."

Bryn leaned up on an elbow and whispered, "I have another favorite. Perhaps a better one for us now is Yeats."

Wine—perhaps Scotch in our case,
Comes in at the mouth
And love comes in at the eye.
That's all we shall know for truth
Before we grow old and die.
I lift the glass to my mouth,
I look at you, and I sigh.

"And, I don't exactly agree with that," he said. "For me, love comes first in the mind."

We heard Steve coming up the stairs. It was nearly midnight.

Bryn leaned over and kissed me and whispered, "Seems we're off on different journeys for now, but maybe we'll meet again someday. I hope so."

The next day I couldn't get my mind off Bryn. We said our goodbyes after breakfast and exchanged emails, but our paths were going in opposite directions, and I didn't expect we would ever see each other again. It wasn't the first time I felt a deep connection with someone I just met. I admit it has only happened a few times. I believe there is an energy between certain people, and we're lucky if enough of those people pass through our lives in one way or another leaving some valuable thought or lesson behind. I am past the idea of soulmates forever—I thought that once, and I was wrong. But I believe there are karmic types of connections that serve as lessons, maybe even harsh ones, and without them we cannot grow. And there is a lesson here. There is no way that enough of those people can pass through our lives unless we expose ourselves often enough to others—to strangers.

I decided to think of Bryn that way—a connection of energies and a lesson learned.

We explored the area; the Blue Ridge Music Center, Humpback Rocks Mountain Farm, and biked the New River Trail to Fries Junction. The Music Center is an amphitheater with a couple of short, easy nature hikes. The Humpback Farm is a group of structures that represent the early farms of the region. I had heard they took down the actual old buildings and moved others for the sake of tourism on the Parkway. I thought the buildings looked out of place, but it's still interesting to see what a one-room cabin at the turn of the century looked like. I can't imagine a large family living in one small room—chopping wood, hauling water, taking baths once a month (I think I heard it was also in the same bathwater), and cooking without a microwave.

The highlight of the day was biking the New River Trail, which is not new; we were told it is one of the oldest in North America. A hiker said the river flows mostly a south to north course, which is against the topology of the area and the west to east flow of most of the other nearby rivers. It's speculated that the river's formation preceded the surrounding landscape.

We cycled on the railway trestles and bridges, picnicked on a rock overlooking the river, and watched the Great Blue Heron fish.

Death by Ivy

Sevierville, Tennessee
to Asheville, North Carolina

It was surprising how many things I had to filter. Three months around the US is the fast-track. No lingering. I had to pick what we considered the highlights for us, and sometimes that had more to do with the route I took and the roadside enticements.

Sevierville was just on the way to somewhere else—just an overnight on our way to Asheville and on to Atlanta. I picked the route just so I could drive through the Great Smoky Mountains.

I had only a vague understanding of Tennessee history, and whatever I had subconsciously recalled had left a taste in my mouth like strong coffee and old cigarettes. The Ku Klux Klan started in Pulaski, the assassination of Martin Luther King in Memphis, home of the atomic bomb in Oak Ridge, and of course, it was the home of Hee Haw, the popular television show of the 1970s, which suggests a level of taste of a good portion of Americans. So many things should outshine these glitches in Tennessee history. Elvis, for one. Jack Daniels, for sure. And then the Great Smokies.

I had taken the long way out of Galax—heading southwest along the ridgeline of the Blue Ridge Parkway through Stone Mountain toward the North Carolina-Tennessee border. As we crossed the border into Tennessee the roads opened up, there was little traffic, small towns, and lots of country music on the radio.

At the Days Inn in Sevierville, I asked what we should see if we were just there for the rest of the afternoon and night. They directed us to the Dolly statue and the Dolly Parton Dixie Stampede at Dollywood in Pigeon Forge just a few miles west.

We decided to see the statue and took a pleasant walk through town. The statue is in front of the courthouse and was smaller than I expected—although, I'm not sure what I expected. Bigger. Bolder. Like Dolly, I guess.

I'm not much of a country music fan, but I like Dolly. She seems like a person I'd like to know. Despite the big hair and pumped-up breasts, she is a woman of substance with a business sense and big heart who keeps returning to her roots to help those less fortunate.

If we were staying another day, I might have gone to Dollywood. I was curious, but we were tired from a long day biking, driving, and stopping at the many overlooks, short trails, and craft shops along the Blue Ridge Parkway.

The next day we headed for Asheville, North Carolina. We took the mountain roads, passing Gatlinburg, Cherokee, and

Dillsboro through the hazy-blue tapestry of the Great Smoky Mountains.

Steve was busy reading a brochure we picked up at the motel in Sevierville.

"Mom, did you know that the bluish haze of the Great Smokies comes from the gases produced by the plants?"

I didn't.

Steve continued his recital from the brochure. "The Smokies are so old that most of their rocks contain only the fossils of the most primitive life forms like trilobites and protozoa, which means the mountains formed in the Precambrian era."

"So, the Smokies were old when the Himalayas were still young? That's good stuff, Steve. You should tell your teacher. I'll bet she would put that into an assignment for your class."

Steve had just started school on the road. It was the first week of testing the new technology with the school. So far, we had exchanged only a couple of emails with the teacher to establish a process for receiving and returning homework assignments.

We stopped twice on the way to Asheville—the Oconaluftee Indian Village and quaint little Dillsboro with its art and craft studios, tree-lined streets, and little white houses. An hour further is Asheville, which seemed like Dillsboro on a larger scale. Art deco buildings, protesters on the corner, drum circle in the park, independent bookstores, coffee shops everywhere, and it seemed like the greenest and lushest place we'd been to on this trip. English ivy, oriental bittersweet, and kudzu vines were about to swallow the town—the entire area. Blankets of green draped everything that didn't move—climbing up and dripping over trees, fences, and poles. They crawled across the road on wires hanging down like party decorations, reshaping the landscape into soft, rounded sculptures. I had a thought that if you ran off the road in certain places, your car would disappear into an ocean of ivy. Death by ivy. I wondered if that had ever happened?

We explored Asheville the next day—the River Arts District and Pritchard Park. The town was growing, and it had the feeling of an organized effort. I wondered how that was sitting with the old locals.

The architecture seemed out of place. Art deco, very modern and yet with European charm and elegance—a strange but interesting convergence for a folksy mountain town.

We discovered that there were many mines along US Highway 441 near Franklin and, according to the signs, the Gem Capital of the World. So, we took a side road into the Pisgah National Forest and Little Switzerland and gem-panned at Emerald Village.

With handfuls of stocked gems, pretty but worthless—we were on our way to Atlanta. The route took us through the corner of South Carolina that welcomed us with a sign—the home of Ms. Kimberly Clarice Aiken, Miss America 1994. I wondered if they considered that to be the highlight of South

Carolina history. Perhaps. She was African American.

Hum, suddenly I was curious. "Hey, Steve? What do you think is beautiful? The sign back there said South Carolina was home to one of the Miss America ladies—so I was wondering what you thought beauty was."

I was disturbing him from the computer game he was playing. He looked up. "What's a Miss America? That sounds like a trick question. You're beautiful, okay? Seriously. Life is beautiful. Now stop bothering me with that stuff."

Great day. He was still a kid.

Road Noise

Signpost on the Road

Atlanta to Savannah, Georgia

It was mid-August and about seven weeks into the trip. Atlanta, like Yellowstone and Portland, Maine, would not turn out as planned, exacerbated by my mood, worry over dwindling money and general claustrophobia being confined to a car for extended periods.

Steve was feeling cooped up, too, and deliberately pushing my buttons. I was driving too much and stopping at too many craft stores. He was eager to get to Florida and the Disney World-Universal Studios thing. And I was anxious to get to the coast again. I needed that feeling of freedom you get when driving along the ocean.

Atlanta held no appeal to me. Looking back, I am not sure why I chose that route. I preferred the small-town experience. Atlanta is a nice enough city—big and beautiful as big cities go, but it was just another big city. Like the rest, Atlanta would be a bricolage of homogeneous big city icons—tall shiny buildings of towering industry. There would also be the assorted accouterments like gourmet restaurants and streets lined with expensive shops and all just a few blocks away from

189

homeless shelters and deteriorating buildings decorated with graffitied statements by artistic but unhappy inhabitants. In Atlanta, there would also be Olympic monuments, statues and museums documenting a proud confederate history, and all surrounded by a beautiful green countryside swept with grand mansions and private golf courses.

It started as soon as I found our way to downtown Atlanta. Steve was navigating with the map, directing me toward the hostel where we planned on staying. After several U-turns and wrong streets, we finally located it in a very questionable part of town. I've stayed at some seedy motels, but this one raised my level of concern for safety.

The hostel looked like a brothel or homeless shelter, and I decided I didn't want to stay there even though I had prepaid. So, we were without a place to stay, and it was getting dark, and I could not get cash from an ATM all day. It had happened before on the trip, but typically in small towns. I thought when I got to Atlanta and some big bank ATMs it wouldn't be a problem. But it was, and my only credit card wasn't working either. We walked to every bank in the downtown area and discovered that none were taking my cards. I was beginning to panic. As usual, Steve was trying to calm me, but I ended up yelling at him, the entire banking system and several clerks that happened to be in my path.

Frantic, I called Wells Fargo Bank from my cell phone while pacing a few back streets in a desperate search for my car. In my emotional turmoil, I had forgotten where I parked. Steve was trying valiantly to save me from myself and ran ahead to look for the car, which only enhanced my anxiety, considering the neighborhood. Several men eyed me strangely from dark doorways as I explained and complained to the bank while calling out to Steve to stay with me. The bank was being cautious; they said. They had put a hold on my accounts because of all the transactions in multiple cities and states. Okay. Then why did they wait seven weeks to do something about it? Maybe they could have called me? They promised to restore access within the hour.

While we waited, we walked to Olympic Park and wet our feet in the fountains. After thirty minutes I tried an ATM and it worked. I took out the money, found the car, and we silently headed south of town. I stopped at the first chain motel, which turned out to be a Motel 6. Within twenty minutes I was showered and sitting on the bed watching television with Steve. I put my head on his shoulder and he patted it like a dog. What a sad, pathetic dog I was.

For the first time on the trip, I was lonely and worried. I knew the mood would pass and that much of the problem was what I had expected since leaving Vermont. The trip down the east coast—with the relentless traffic, congestion, and people everywhere, city after city, would get to me. Getting to Florida would lift my spirits and Steve's.

Outside Savannah, I got off Highway 95 for the coastal route of Florida's A1A. I wound around through Fernandina Beach and Amelia City and into Neptune Beach. It was along this stretch that I began to see signs, flags, and posters of Jerry Garcia (Grateful Dead). A large purple one hung from the walls of a surf shop, *Thank you, Jerry.* Having been out of touch with the news, I soon found out that Garcia had died a few days prior on August 9.

I was never a hippie or a Deadhead, but I was a sympathizer. I understood the appeal of misfit power—a collaboration that embraces and shapes its environment and yet provides space for each to be its own.

Most Deadheads I know are second generation—too young to know the 1960s and even much of the 1970s, but then, it was never an age thing with the *Dead.* It was a commonality of utopian ideals, not always realized but strived for, that drew them to the music where they found acceptance. Every concert was a family reunion and not just of concert-goers but with the band, the staff, and the ticket-takers, and that was a direction the band took from the very beginning. They knew the experience could only be complete if every concert called up the commonality and dependence between them all. Corporate America could learn a thing or two from Deadhead philosophy.

I wondered about the *spinners,* though—those of any belief system or community that conform with such singular devotion to something or someone in a world that is so random and uncontrollable. What we do now—will it mean anything? Really? Garcia didn't think so.

For me, there was no time in the 1970s for such concepts. I was in my early twenties, divorced with a full-time job making only enough to scrape by. By the late 1970s, I was dating the man that would become my son's father and developing a tendency toward a yuppie lifestyle that didn't suit my Deadism philosophy, but it was better than being constantly broke. I sold out I suppose.

After a few side roads, detours, and dead ends that led through several state parks, I ended up in Neptune Beach. We stopped at a pizza place on Beach Street and decided we would stay around for another day.

Garcia would have said it was a *meaningful coincidence and a signpost on the road.*

Road Noise

Deep Blue

Jacksonville Beach, Florida

My first anxiety attack was in 1986. I was at the nasty beginning of a traumatic divorce that would last nearly two years for the first round, and then a second custody battle two years later. Anxiety and panic attacks in those early years were confusing and terrifying. More than once I ended up in the ER thinking I was having a heart attack. Years later, I figured out a few ways to control the panic. I would start by demanding to myself in my head to stop, but sometimes I found myself uttering the words out loud and that wouldn't do in a work environment. I later realized it was more effective to wear a rubber band around my wrist, and when I felt an attack coming on, I gave myself a good snap. Other times I would snap my fingers with my arm down at my side or behind my back so that others couldn't see. If the panic didn't subside quickly, I would have to move to a quiet room and shut the door.

In late 1989, I became involved with Jason, the man who put much of that to rest for a while. He calmed and comforted me but by early 1993 his own demons surfaced, and although they had nothing to do with me, our relationship came to a slow, agonizing end, leaving us both still in love but unable to conquer the beasts of his PTSD.

In mid-1993, just two years before this road trip, I started deep visualizations—a way of reprogramming my mind to tame the noise and negative chatter in my head. I had developed my own technique and even led a meditation group for a while. My visualizations took me and my group *up* into higher consciousness, beyond body mindfulness. My favorite visualization, the one I did most often I called *Deep Blue* and could take as long as an hour.

In my mind, I went to a stretch of beach where the water was warm. I closed my eyes and would imagine myself in the water, floating effortlessly—the water suspending me. I felt the water on my skin and slowly the water and my body would become the same temperature until I felt as if I became part of the water. After a few more minutes, I would begin to feel my body dissolve, leaving my consciousness as part of the water. The feeling was that of release, like boundaries had been removed. There was a freedom and yet it felt like a safe place, and I could linger there for a long time.

· · ·

Jacksonville Beach looked enough like my *Deep Blue* beach that I felt a sudden comfort and calm. Steve was eager to get to Orlando, but seeing the ocean again was a welcome sight. We both needed some time out of the car and some sand in our toes. Although the sunshine was scarce, southern hospitality was abundant.

Within ten minutes of checking into the motel, we headed for the beach. I had my book and Pink Floyd on headphones. Steve found two kids and a dog that wanted to play. The kids, a girl about nine and her younger brother, were delighted to have another playmate.

The dog was a hyper-bouncing small tan and white ankle-licker being held on a leopard patterned leash by a tall woman in her mid-thirties. I tried desperately to avoid the licking by lifting my feet off the sand.

The woman sensed my annoyance, "Oh, sorry. She won't bite, but for some reason, she loves people's feet." She threw a treat so the dog would leave me alone. "Do you mind if I put my chair here? I see our kids are playing together. I'm glad. Mine need a break from each other. We've been having a bit of sibling rivalry lately, and I might just have to put one of 'em in the trunk for the ride home."

I laughed, "Of course. Please, sit."

The mother of the dog and the kids was Dina. We sat near the water's edge on Jacksonville Beach kid-watching, talking, and drinking sweet tea. Dina was a beauty with dark wavy hair, creamy southern skin, a slim, curvy figure, and a North Carolina voice as sweet and gentle as pansies on the porch.

She talked of her new man with a decided softness, claiming she was in love for the second time in her life. We had a lot in common as we talked of past relationships and our mutual interest in men with an adventurous spirit.

Dina laughed with a sweet childlike giggle, "Like what? What would be your ideal adventurous man?"

"Humm. Maybe someone like Denys from *Out of Africa*— a man who bravely embraces and defends nature but can't be tamed. A purist in nature and in love. And you?"

"My first marriage was to a mountain guide in Alaska where I lived for a few years with my father, who was stationed up there. I was young, barely in my twenties when I met Connor who guided expeditions up Denali. He was older than me but so adventurous, fearless, and handsome. I was over the moon infatuated. Adventurous types may be exciting, but I don't think they make great husbands. Connor didn't and turned out to be physically abusive."

"Oh, I'm sorry," I said. "Well, maybe something not quite that adventurous this time. What does your new man do?"

She giggled again, "He's an accountant."

She said she started to pray a couple of years ago to help extricate herself from the bad relationship and find her way to a good man. She said it worked. Not long after, she ran into an old friend who fell back into her life—this time, as a lover.

Skeptical me, I suspect she would have run into the old friend anyway and god got undue credit but, I must admit, I have not tried praying for a man. I just don't think any proper god would concern himself with relationship problems. These are his trivial pursuits? Aren't there bigger fish to fry? If we pray, should we not be praying for the big stuff—orphans, children with cancer, war veterans without legs? World peace?

But those thoughts swirled only in my head for a few seconds. I liked her and her charming children and I was happy she found love again and I hoped I would get to meet this nice young man.

I looked up to see a man standing in the shallow edge of the waves addressing her kids. Balding, belly paunch, about five foot six and mid-forties. I knew from his tone who he was—the fiancé.

"Time to get out. We're going to dinner. Let's go. Let's go!"

He was clapping his hands together to get their attention over the slurping waves and children's laughter. I heard myself sigh in my head. These days, I am a love-skeptic, but I kept my negativity in check and wished nothing but the best for Dina. All my heroes turned into ghosts, but hers might not. I am frequently wrong and can't be trusted to provide relationship advice, and she reminded me that love happens when you least expect it and when your guard is down and when you meditate or perhaps pray for it. But who can tell?

So, so you think you can tell
Heaven from hell?

Road Noise

Taking a Ride

Orlando, Florida

Storms that were lining up in the Gulf forced me to skip the Keys and southern Florida. It was probably just as well as I would have spent too much money and probably tossed back more than a few margaritas at beachside bars, and this wasn't the trip for that.

Instead, I swung the car west out of Daytona and headed for Orlando. The next several days were all Steve's. If he wanted to eat an ice cream cone as big as his head, have cotton candy for dinner, go on the same ride thirty-five times, or play arcade games until midnight—okay. In Orlando, I was just along for the ride.

Orlando is an inverse of nature. Reality eliminated. I have an aversion to everything about amusement parks and similar activities that involve confined quarters with lots of people and chaos, and that includes Las Vegas and cruise ships. I find amusement parks to be a personal assault from every direction; the noise, crowds, lines, cost, the pedestrian accouterments, the dumbing-down, the bad food. And did I mention the screaming kids and forced proximity to thousands of people at the same time? But that aside, I wanted the opportunity to re-explore magic and fantasy again and have a bit of simple fun with Steve.

There was just one problem. I was over budget, having spent too much in Boston and New York City. I was counting dollars and had allocated each one for all the upcoming activities for the next two weeks. There was little to spare. I had a backup credit card, but it didn't have much of a limit and I was trying to keep that for emergencies. I knew once we got into the park, I would need more money and I was having anxiety on the drive to Orlando.

I had already made reservations at the Palm Lakefront Hostel on Lake Cecile in Kissimmee, just minutes from Orlando. It was on the Highway 192 strip which I knew had unlimited sensory entertainment, most of it not to my taste, but I knew Steve would love it and it would be interesting if just to see how many bright lights, arcades, go-kart tracks, and whirling rides can be squeezed into a block-size strip-mall.

Driving toward Kissimmee, I saw signs for timeshares offering free ticket packages to the parks if you attended one of the morning sales sessions. Perfect. I could do that. Two free tickets to two parks and a couple of lunch passes would save me about $300! I was familiar with the hard sell tactics and knew what I would be getting into. The sessions started at 8 AM every morning and claimed to last only two hours.

The Palm Lakefront Hostel was converted from an old resort motel and was one of the better places we stayed the entire trip. There was nothing fancy about the rooms, but they were clean and nice. It was close to everything, backed up to the lake with a dock and paddleboats, and had a nice pool and well-kept grounds full of lizards, much to Steve's delight. He caught several that seemed content to hang on his shirt while he searched for more.

The weather was hot and misty through most of our stay, with occasional light rain that came and went and didn't hamper our activities. The next day would be my sales session at the condos and in the afternoon, Universal Studios. The following day we would do Disney/MGM Studios followed by Sea World. In the evening it would be go-karts and arcades in Old Town.

The next morning, I was up early, gulped down two cups of coffee and told Steve I would be back in a couple of hours with my usual demand that he not leave the property but already knowing that he wouldn't. Steve had always followed the rules, but as a precaution, I had already spoken to the motel manager and prepaid a housekeeper to keep an eye on my room and Steve, but I didn't tell him that.

At the timeshare session, I knew I was going to get accosted by more than one salesperson, and I knew they were hard closers. They would use several tactics I was familiar with, having spent all my career working closely with salespeople. I had prepared a strategy and in the initial interview; I was clear to ask how long the process would take, and if I was obligated in any way. He said it would take about sixty minutes (it took nearly two hours) and that I was under no obligation. Of course, they asked me all the questions about being a single woman there. Where was my husband? I assured the initial interviewer that I didn't have a husband and was financially independent. I was convincing and made it past the initial interview to face the closer teams.

The first ten minutes was a group presentation, just marketing hype with a very charismatic and handsome host. Stunning property photos hung on the walls and eight beautiful salespeople wandered the room smiling and handing out packets of information. They were assessing us, picking out which salesperson would go for which potential buyer. The handsome host played a video showing all the benefits physically and financially while showing dozens of smiling, happy couples enjoying their well-spent money at this lovely place in sunny Florida.

After the group presentation, I was approached by the first salesman, a man named Sidney. He seemed about thirty-five years old with a bronze tan, blond and well-groomed hair, and wearing a navy blazer and tan pants; he looked like he should have been on the deck of a yacht. He was flirty and funny and made a point of telling me he was single and loved living in Florida. At first, he made lots of casual conversation. Just more assessment, I thought. After a typical sales pitch, I made it clear that I loved the idea of a timeshare, but I would not be purchasing or signing anything today and that I never bought anything on impulse. He said he was just there to help, then he took my hand like a princess, kissed it, and said a sweet goodbye and I found myself standing alone. A minute later I was approached by another salesman who offered me some Florida orange juice in a champagne glass and a small plate of chocolate-covered strawberries. Andrew was a little older, mid-forties maybe, and more sophisticated looking, a classic white shirt and suit guy. He pitched the money angle.

"Do you ever take vacations?"

"Sure," I said. Then he got me to chatting about the last one to Maui.

"What would you say if you took that same amount of money and guaranteed that not only would you stay in a beautiful place every year, but that the next three generations of your family including your son and his children would also have access to this flexible plan?"

Three generations? I again repeated my comment about loving the condos but not buying on impulse, and after fifteen minutes Andrew left. A few minutes later, a woman approached me. She had a new tactic and attempted to appeal to my independent you-go-girl side. This cycle went on through a few more sales pitches, some more appealing than others, and I admit there was a part of me that, for a moment, thought it would be nice to have a timeshare in Florida. I reminded myself what I was there for and eventually; I was given my vouchers and released.

I got back to the Palm and found Steve at the lake's edge with six lizards clinging to his shirt. He was smiling ear to ear.

"Hey, Mom, where have you been? I've been teaching Jenny how to catch lizards." He motioned to a girl with a blonde ponytail and pink sundress who was bent down with her hand in the water at the edge of the shallow lake.

"That's excellent. I left you a note that I went to a timeshare. Didn't you see it?"

"Yeah, I saw the note I just don't know what a timeshare is."

"Oh, never mind about that. Are you ready to go to Universal Studios?

After two days and long hours of theme park stimulation, I got mixed up which movie-themed rides and shows were at which place, but Steve knew and remembered the details of every ride and exhibit and recounted every one for the next few days.

Wild Life

Tampa, Apalachicola and
Panama City Beach, Florida

The sun rolled over the last cloud in the sky opening up the wide blue before us. It was 6 AM, my favorite time of day to drive. I had coffee in one hand, steering with the other, shades on, and watching the yellow shadows slowly fade up into blue.

Slurping straw sounds indicated Steve had just finished his second apple juice box. We were both hyped up on the residual energy of Orlando and ready to visit Tampa to observe the imprisoned aquatic life at the Florida Aquarium. We loved all types of zoos, aquariums, wild animal parks, and even roadside petting zoos and would stop at any that came near our route. We had already visited many on this trip. Our favorite so far was the Shedd Aquarium in Chicago that had the albino alligator.

As long as we provide them a big cell, a good health plan, and social security, then I'm okay imprisoning most types (not all) of wildlife so the masses have something to do besides sit in front of a television watching sports or cooking shows.

But I have a few requests on their behalf:

Please don't hobble me to keep me
If I can fly, don't clip my wings
If I need to roam, don't chain me
Don't cut back my teeth or claws
Don't take my babies from me
Don't keep me from others of my kind

The Florida Aquarium was nicely done but small, so we went through it twice. Steve was staring at a large grouper with bulging eyes. He and another kid were tapping on the glass. The grouper looked straight at the boys and hovered for a while in front of them.

A woman who clearly worked there leaned over to them, "That's Cleatus, he's a goliath grouper. He may not look that bright, but groupers are about as smart as a dog. He's sizing you up. I think he likes you."

"He's cool. I don't think he looks dumb. I think he's thinking," said Steve. "Is he friendly?"

"He seems friendly enough, but he's young and new here, so we'll wait and see. We're all new here. The aquarium just opened."

I was now listening in on their conversation, "Just opened?"

"Yes, the aquarium just opened a few months ago. It's small now, but it's going to grow."

I gave her a big smile. She was friendly and so happy to be there, and so were we. It's so comforting to meet people who enjoy their jobs and take pride in their work and then take the time to share that joy with others. *I don't do that very often. I should.*

"How exciting to be at the birth of a new aquarium," I said. "We used to live in Carmel and visited the Monterey Bay Aquarium all the time. Literally. Season ticket holders. When Steve was a toddler, I would take him there almost every afternoon. It calmed him down—and me, too. Good luck to you and the aquarium."

Steve was particularly fond of reptiles and insects so, on the way out, we bought the *Audubon Field Guide to Reptiles and Amphibians* at the gift shop. He studied that book from cover to cover over and over from the time we left Tampa all the way through Phoenix.

It had been a long day in Tampa. We were tired, but I prefer to stay in small towns where it's easier to get around, so I drove north until dinner time, which took us into Perry, Florida.

It was a strange little town—wind-battered (or maybe that's just the way it looked), surrounded by swamp, rundown, seemed nearly deserted, and there was an odor in the air I couldn't put my nose around. At a gas station, I asked a forty-something man in a baseball cap what there was to see in Perry and where we might stay the night.

"Also, am I crazy or do I smell something?"

He chuckled and smiled, "It's the paper mill in town. I've gotten used to it, but a lot of people never do."

"It's a very odd smell, isn't it?"

"Odd and bad! To me it is sort of a metallic sulphury smell. The mill is pretty much the only place to work around here, so a lot of people don't stick around. As far as a place to stay, Gandy Motor Lodge is decent. Not much to do around here. You might want to look at the Cracker houses. A lot of people find those interesting. Can't miss 'em, they're all over the place."

"Cracker house?"

"Yeah, that's what they call 'em. It's a distinct style of a house built by early settlers of the area."

We spotted several Cracker houses along the road. They seemed to be oddly located like they'd been moved there— perhaps for tourism? I pulled over, and we walked through a couple of them. They seemed to me to be quite inventive. They were built to take advantage of cross breezes for ventilation in the days before air conditioning. They were usually raised or set on blocks to allow airflow underneath. The ones we saw had two small rooms separated by a breezeway and had a large, covered porch that went around much of the house. And then I noticed the gaps in the floorboards.

. . .

My father used to tell stories of his missionary work around Apalachicola in the 1940s. They were strange stories any kid would remember. Rundown houses on stilts with floorboards so wide apart the family table scraps were just dropped through for the pigs that roamed freely underneath. We just found out they called these Cracker houses.

The tourist books call it Florida's forgotten coast. It was mostly a weather-battered one-lane road along the coast from Sopchoppy to Apalachicola. We stopped several times to explore the coastline. Little sand was left—and only remnants of structures that once stood in the way of a hurricane. All that remained were pieces of rusted metal, cement slabs, and crumbling brick fireplaces wrapped with parts of trees. We explored what was left of the beachfront and I took pictures of the brown pelicans that perched on piers just off the shore— piers that used to be trees or parts of houses.

All along the road were rundown, weather-beaten houses that looked abandoned—many were barely standing. I decided to stop and take some pictures. Steve was strongly objecting, claiming that people were living there.

"Mom. We need to go. People live here."

"No way," I said, my eye still against the camera's viewfinder.

"Mom. There's a man on the porch behind you."

I glanced around and was horrified. A tall, thin man in a white undershirt had come out to the porch and was looking at me. Someone lived there!

Oh god, someone lived there. Almost every window was broken. The door was hanging twisted—no way it closed.

There were only two broken cement steps where there should have been three. The house was tilted, twisted like it had been pulled around toward the sea. The surrounding yard (if you could call it that) was full of trash and overgrowth that had been there for a long time. There were no cars or bikes or vehicles—just scraps of metal strewn around like broken toys.

Without saying anything, we slouched to the car and left.

"Sorry. You were right. Should I go back and apologize? What would I say? Oh my god."

"No, just leave it. I told you," Steve said.

We drove in silence for the next thirty minutes.

We pulled into Panama City Beach at about noon. You would have to be dead not to know its primary existence is to accommodate the spring break party crowd. And why not? Thirty miles of quartz sand so fine and white that it squeaked under-foot and turquoise blue water surrounded by air so warm that wearing anything but flip-flops bordered on the absurd. There was a bar on every corner that stood next to a gift shop that sold beer koozies, bikinis so small they could only fit breasts that stood up and waved, and T-shirts that said *I've fallen, and I can't find my beer.*

The Days Inn was oceanfront with a couple of waterfalls that cascaded over rocks into a stunning pool. The managers were friendly and gave me a special deal and a room with a kitchenette. It was off season, so I figured any guests were special guests. We were steps away from the beach The temperature was 85 degrees, and the sky was bright blue without a cloud insight. We unpacked the minimum, changed into swimming gear, and went straight to the beach.

Almost immediately Steve found a boy his age to body surf with until dark. His parents and I struck up a conversation and sat on a deck overlooking the boys until nearly midnight.

Rick and Cheryl were traveling gospel singers from Pascagoula, Mississippi. He was mid-forties and she, thirty-six. Only a few years ago they were drowning in booze. They met, dried up, found religion, and began a life of professional singing. By trade, Cheryl was a geologist. She shared tips on where to find gemstones in the upcoming weeks of our trip.

We stayed another day to play in the surf and relax. Steve and his new friend body surfed to exhaustion, and I watched the waves slide and roll over glistening white sand. In between reading *Shooting the Boh*, hypnotic wave-watching, and monitoring the boys, I photographed pelicans diving for fish.

As evening fell, a deep purple sky immersed us and a blend of orange, pink, and yellow slid across the horizon and crystal beams shimmered on the water. A tiny memory came back from my childhood.

We were at someone's beachfront house that had panoramic glass windows in the front and wooden steps that took us down onto twilight pink sand only steps from a dark sea. I see a deep purple sky and feel a damp mist on my face. My lavender Sunday dress floats above several petticoats. Stern words from my mother come down from the deck, "Don't get her dress wet." I feel my father's hand as we laugh and play in the surf. Then, handfuls of sand and a dress dripping with ocean color. My father and I were laughing. Mommy would be mad.

Eyes of the Swamp

New Orleans and Slidell, Louisiana

The Louisiana bayou is minimalistic—primal life stripped of embellishments. No hesitations. Act or die. Discover that place at the root of you where everything you need already exists. That is the swamp, and in another way, that is New Orleans.

The Louisiana Honey Island Swamp is a place where the zeitgeist is as pure as it was ten millennia ago. One of the least-altered swamps in the US, its complexity is still evolving.

Memories of New Orleans were recent—only a few years previously and involved significant amounts of alcohol, music, and men. For a couple of decades, I was the only female—the marketing director at several technology companies. I worked with salespeople pushing software for things quite useful, like hierarchical databases, data mining, and telemedicine. It was a time that I loved business travel—something similar in excitement to late-night dates when I was seventeen—the exhilaration of being away from home.

New Orleans is a trade show destination, and those who attend spend far more time drunk and disabled than pitching products. I once spent two weeks exhibiting at back-to-back trade shows, organizing for, and entertaining clients, media people, and various company salespeople. By the time I left, I had a persistent toxic-booze headache, gut-rot from all the fried and edgy food, and such fatigue that I slept on the plane and for two days after.

Of all the times I had been to New Orleans on business, I had never done the one thing I wanted to do. None of my business colleagues were interested in a swamp tour. But this trip, our first stop would be Slidell to tour the bayou.

After two days on the Panama City Beach sand, we were ready to do something different. I dashed through Alabama and Mississippi, arriving midafternoon in Slidell. I found a motel and quickly got on the phone to find a tour company—which turned out to be Gator Swamp Tours in the Honey Island Swamp on the Pearl River. Danny was just what I was hoping for—no Hollywood tour set, no air-conditioned covered boat, no over-marketed hype—just the same simplicity that exudes from every sweating pore of the swamp.

Danny owned and ran Gator Swamp Tours. He was a Louisiana caricature. He and his wife lived on a houseboat that sat permanently at the edge of the swamp. The two-story boat was about the size of a compact two-bedroom apartment with a deck that ran the circle of the boat and overlooked the murky water of the Pearl River. Portside was a wood plank gated walkway to the shore to keep assorted animals—wild boar, deer, cougars—off the boat. Off stern was a dock where he put in a narrow uncovered boat that looked to be about twenty-five feet long. Running loose on the shore was a goat, a dozen chickens, an ill-tempered rooster, a timorous shore-bound duck that didn't go in the water because he was afraid of alligators, a friendly potbellied pig, and a nutria which looked like a beaver-rat combo with the disposition of a cat (if gently raised). Flanking the boat throughout the day and night—were alligators of various sizes. They all looked friendly enough, calmly floating not far away from the boat, looking for food that might fall off, one way or another.

Our swamp tour started at 11 AM. It was late August and hot. Only two other couples were on the tour—seven people in the boat without gear, counting Captain Danny.

"I'm going to turn on a little AC," he said. We all looked at each other. It was an open canoe.

"Hold on." Suddenly, he punched the accelerator, and with a lurch forward a warm but refreshing Louisiana breeze hit our faces.

We sped along the main waterway for about a mile passing rundown covered fishing shacks that can be rented Danny said, for some 'sweet-talk and promises.'

We swung starboard into a narrow slough. The Honey Island Swamp is a maze of them. Dense vegetation pushed out from the banks, providing luxurious cover for alligators and snakes observing from the muddy edge. Spanish moss hung over the water from the branches of cypress and tupelo trees.

"Watch out for snakes in those low-hanging branches.
And watch for the cutgrass along the sides of the boat. It's pretty sharp."

Life on a houseboat at the edge of a swamp comes with its own set of rules and demands wisdom that only comes with a savvy understanding of your environment. Danny hunted everything and said he would eat anything that didn't eat him first. He didn't have the appearance of a back-land naturalist; he looked more like a city dweller turned zoologist with his slim physique and tailored hair and beard.

Danny grew up in Slidell and knew how to maneuver the swamp. He knew that the oak and pine trees grew only on dry ground. He knew which plants were edible—arrowroot, sweet pea, bay leaves, wild rice, and black willow, and which snakes to honor a right-of-way. He could smell if a wild boar were near and tell which fish were spawning in the banks. He was a man who had earned his time there and respected the subordination and hierarchy of the swamp.

At the end of the tour, the nutria was waiting for us on the dock. She was familiar with the routine and surveyed the boat for fish. She quickly found the gar that Danny had pulled out of the water and nibbled its long nose. Steve had run off to the animals looking for the pig. Danny asked about our trip, and I asked him what it was like on the swamp at night.

"Why don't I show you? You and Steve can stay with us tonight and I'll take you out after dinner. You'll like the swamp at night. It's a whole other world."

There was no hesitation to take him up on the offer. At 9 PM the three of us set out on the boat again. After a mile or so, Danny shut off the navigation light. The moon was bright and cast a dim light on the dark water. He slowed the boat to a crawl and navigated to a narrow slough. We were only about eight feet from the bank on either side.

Danny handed each of us a flashlight. "Now, skim your lights along the bank and surface of the water."

Among the dark safety of the spider lilies, Louisiana iris, bald cypress, tupelo gum, willow, and palmettos were white, red, and golden eyes reflecting from all directions. The water, the banks, and the trees were alive.

Danny turned off the engine, and we sat rocking in the shallow water staring at the eyes staring at us. Steve was silent as he ran his flashlight along the banks, catching several pairs of reflecting eyes every time he moved the light. It was both cartoonish and frightening at the same time. The throaty rattle of frogs interrupted the stillness and the harmonious choir of crickets. Every few minutes you could hear a rustle in the brush or quick ripples on the water. From the banks, deer, wild boar, raccoons, cougars, snakes, and spiders were watching not far away. From the water, snakes and alligators were aware of our presence. We were being observed.

Humans and their boats were a common sight and one to be wary of during the day, but the night belonged to them. We were the trespassers. One slip-up and the advantage of our size could be irrelevant. All that stood between us and them was a floating piece of aluminum rocking gently on the murky water.

The engine started up. "Let's take her to the big water."

The boat sped off, curving around narrows and bends in the river, barely missing branches sprawling over the shallow slough. Within minutes we were at the edge of Lake Pontchartrain, which spread in front of us like an ocean. He stopped the engine. We sat quietly and listened—the only sounds were the distant vibrations of human interference and the slow-moving ripples that sucked against the boat. Steve was never as still and quiet as he was that night.

Next stop, New Orleans to listen to street music and visit the Aquarium of the Americas. We loved the shark tank that housed some of the biggest sharks held in captivity, sea turtles, stingrays, and jellies. Steve found two kids about his age almost immediately. They were there with their grandparents from London, who seemed delighted to have Steve help entertain them.

"Hey, Mom! Jonathan just tapped on that glass and the pufferfish got all puffed!"

"Good thing he's incarcerated."

Let's Mess with Texas

Houston to San Antonio, Texas

Right or wrong, our memories from places we've lived permanently shape our views of them. A lot of perfectly nice places get a bad rap. California for one.

I wasn't born in California but spent the better part of my life fighting the traffic and cost of living and yet letting out a big *ahhhh* every time I sank into the big comfortable couch that it is.

If you are from California, you are not necessarily a crack-smoking, tree-hugging, liberal, gay, porn-star. And so, I guess I owe that line of thought to Texas. Not all Texans, I suppose, are beer-swilling, Bambi-killing, finger-waving, egomaniacs. They can't be.

I only lived in Houston for two years, but it felt like a lifetime. During that time, there were two in-law family tragedies (teen suicide and a head-on fatal collision with an underage intoxicated driver), a trip to the ER, an in-law family business in shambles, drugs, alcohol, and a lot of attitude. But it didn't end there. I was employed by a company where everybody cheated and/or hit-on everybody, and every Friday night was happy hour that started at the office. It was common to see two people going at it in the copy room. Driving drunk was just part of a normal day or night, rifle racks, road rage, death threats, bank theft, pay-offs—all of this happened in some way related to me and not of my own doing. And I lived in the nice part of town.

I'm not even going to bore you with the problems in my marriage—of course, with all that happening, it stands to reason our marriage would have been a mess in Texas, too. I know this stuff goes on everywhere, but never had I experienced so much trouble from all different angles, in such a small timeframe and in such a big place. Was it just an unlucky two years? Or does Texas just breed this kind of chaos? Maybe a bit of both. There's more.

My first weekend in Houston, I experienced blue laws. Seriously? I needed to buy pantyhose for a job interview the next day. No. Couldn't. Blue laws.

My first day on the job at a local bank; a young hot cowboy walks in—cowboy boots, big shiny bullhorn belt, the whole look—sits down at my desk, puts his dirty cowboy boots on my desk facing me (I kid you not) and says, "We should go out." That was his opening line. Really? Maybe in Texas women like that kind of arrogance?

Leaving Texas two years later with my husband: We were almost out—not far from El Paso, around Van Horn, when we were stopped for speeding (we weren't) along an incredibly boring stretch of Highway 10. Good thing we had $300 in cash on us. The officer asked how much cash we had on us and ironically that was the same amount as the speeding ticket. Just pay the officer, and we were on our way.

So, admittedly, my taste for Texas on our three-month cross-country trip was kin to Texas sour crude. I didn't plan to linger, but it's a big state that requires a lot of careful driving just to get from one end to the other. I had already warned Steve, as we were leaving New Orleans, that the next two days would be a lot of car-time so buckle into the headphones and video games.

One of the most boring drives on the entire trip was the long straight road between Houston and San Antonio. Then there were the bugs, more bugs, and then some really big bugs. I had to stop several times to clean bug guts off my window so I could see to drive. You think I'm exaggerating, but you would be wrong.

As we got close to San Antonio, I saw a sign for a wild animal safari park—a drive-through type that Steve and I love. So, we detoured toward New Braunfels for the Natural Bridges Wildlife Ranch. Giraffes, elephants, zebras, rhinoceros, ostriches—excellent!

· · ·

The manager of the Crocket Hotel, which sits steps away from the Alamo and only two blocks to the River Walk, offered me a room at a reduced rate that was too good to pass up. I think Steve had charmed her. When I brought the bags inside, he was showing her his recent foreign money acquisitions. Suddenly her head whipped back in laughter.

"He's telling me all about your trip! You two are quite the adventurers."

She was mussing his hair and beaming at Steve and in her sweet Texas accent she said, "Well, I am going to see to it you enjoy your stay in San Antonio, even if you won't be here that long!"

Hey. There's a nice thing to say about Texas. Yes, the people are friendly. They like Texas and they really want you to like it, too.

It was a beautiful sunny afternoon. A little hot, but that was to be expected. We dropped the bags in the room and walked to the Alamo. Steve was in virtual school now, and his teacher back home had worked some lessons around his travels, including one about the Alamo. Our visit was more than just a tourist visit—it required Steve to take some notes for a test he would receive via email later in the day. Although he was not one for history, he enjoyed seeing history that way— connecting real visuals with facts, names, and dates.

I had been to San Antonio four times before on business trade shows. San Antonio is a great trade show destination— everything is all confined to a walking area of a mile or two— a charming walk along a river all lit up with lights like it's Christmas year-round. Other trade show essentials were all-around—plenty of overpriced shops for those who ruin their business clothing while partying, bars and restaurants that stay open late, live music everywhere to keep people awake, drinking and dancing, and discrete hotel staff never assuming the person hanging from someone's arm is a spouse. What happens at trade shows gets torn down and discarded with the debris. And so, another nice thing to say about Texas. San Antonio is charming, fun and would be a delightful place to go with or without a trade show.

I wanted to stroll the River Walk. Steve was bored and delighted when I suggested he go back to the room, which allowed me time to have a scotch-rocks, sit along the river and people watch.

The man at the next table was about my age with dark wavy hair that looked wet, and I was deciding whether he had just gotten out of the shower or was using too much hair slick. Either way, he was extremely attractive with high cheekbones, a broad smile with perfectly aligned teeth, dark skin, and thick eyelashes over brown eyes. He was the exotic-looking type. *Was he an adventurer or a flamenco dancer?* He was wearing a dark long sleeve shirt tucked into slim jeans and had on nice shoes. I was happy they weren't cowboy boots.

I smiled at him. I don't usually do that—smile at strangers. It's not that I don't want to be friendly, I just don't always want to engage in casual conversation about the weather. I'm an introvert and that attitude or personality trait, whatever name we want to call it—some might say bitchy, but that's not true. Regardless, it has not served me well, and early in the trip I tried to step out of that habit. Sometimes I just wanted to sit alone and think, but that warm peaceful night after a couple of scotches and all alone beside that pretty river with the Christmas lights in the trees throwing delicate shadows, I felt like being friendly. Of course, smiling at a man is an immediate invitation, and he didn't hesitate and started off with the best opening line I'd heard in years—maybe ever.

"The lights around your hair make you look like an angel. Are you?"

I felt myself flush. I think my face got pink. I searched my brain but could not think of one clever thing to say to that, so I giggled and said thank you.

His name was Adam and after some casual chit-chat about why I was in San Antonio and giving my usual condensed version of my three-month journey with my son, I asked where he was from and why he was in town.

"Born and raised in Houston, but I've lived in many places. My favorite is Santorini. I'm a sommelier which allowed me to travel a bit. But that's not why I'm here."

Suddenly I liked him even more, "I hate to tell you this, but I know pretty much nothing about wine other than I prefer it dry and white. I'm really more of a scotch drinker. But, if it matters, I'm a bit of a scotch connoisseur. My motto is life's too short for cheap booze. So why are you here then?"

He laughed, "I'm writing a book about dating—I don't have a title yet, but it's focused on women, how to get a guy interested. I don't want that to sound creepy, but the dating world is not for the timid. I have four sisters and I hear their painful relationship problems all the time. And after each break up, they sit at home wishing for mister perfect to show up on the doorstep instead of getting back out there. They come to me for advice. I'm not sure why, but other women seem to want my opinion, too. So, I started writing it all down. I tell them, if you want to meet the right man, you have to get out of the house and leave your stress and fears behind."

Of all the things I had expected him to be—a salesman, a local musician, or perhaps the owner of one of the River Walk shops, a dating self-help author was last on my list.

"I sound just like your sisters—divorced twice, and I've pretty much given up. Besides getting out of the house, what's your advice for me?"

"There are a couple things divorced women do that don't help them. They think it's about children, that having kids turns men off and for most good men that's not true. But here are a couple things I keep hearing. Men don't want to hear about your past relationships. Never say anything bad about a previous husband or boyfriend. Save all that for some far future conversation. And don't be afraid to flirt but do it sweetly. When you flirt, you're in control, you can turn it on or off at any moment, but at least you started the momentum."

We bantered back and forth for two more hours, and his advice was solid. His tips included: find a similarity, if you're interested say so, and allow yourself to be funny. *Not so strangely, I thought, I don't currently do any of those things. Maybe he was right. Maybe that's why I'm still single.*

I would have thought there was an arrogance behind his charm, but there wasn't. He seemed sensitive and genuine.

It was nearly midnight when I got back to the room. I had a feeling of euphoria. I enjoyed meeting Adam. I checked on Steve, who had fallen asleep with the television on and the laptop on the bed. I went back outside to sit in the warm night air for a few more minutes. I was glad I had smiled at Adam. A lesson from my encounter with Bryn. I allowed another stranger to pass through my life.

I sat on a white plastic chair just outside the room with a bottle of water. I was alone except for an incredibly large cockroach that scurried past my foot, oblivious to my watchful eye. He didn't touch me, so I allowed him to live.

The birds chirped. The air was warm. I closed my eyes and could imagine I was on Santorini—except for the hum of the air conditioners above and the faint smell of fish from the waterfall pond. I was relaxed and peaceful. And yet another thing nice to say about Texas.

Serendipity

Carlsbad, New Mexico

The drive to Fort Stockton got off to a late start. Three of four times on this trip, the FedEx package that was to arrive by 10:30 AM was late. The packages were usually my mail—bills that needed to be paid—things I didn't want to leave behind at some motel. At least, it was a typical San Antonio morning. The air was warm and the sky solid blue. Steve was still asleep. No sense waking him, I was enjoying the quiet.

I left Steve a note—a Post It on the bathroom door and a pen dropped on the floor. It was, and remains, our message-methodology. I walked to the River Walk, found some coffee and a bench near the water where the sun rays would beat hard on my stiff shoulders. I watched the murky river slurp against the rock walls and waited another hour for the package that never came.

Only a few things were a hassle on this trip that didn't involve my own stupidity, like locking the keys in the car in Nebraska, and top of the list, was the untimely FedEx deliveries that, not only wasted my time with numerous phone calls but caused me frustrated concern about leaving behind a package with my name, address, and bills with credit card numbers. Other annoying things on this trip were almost all traffic-related—missing, confusing, or absurdly placed road signs, road construction, and the incredible traffic in the coastal Northeast (and I thought Southern California was bad). But we had left all that. We were in the open now—a quick marathon through Texas heading back west following the blank colorless spaces—the places where coyotes, lizards, ants, scorpions, and snakes out-number human life. I was happy about that.

Sun daggers were stabbing at my shoulders, and an influx of lunch-goers were crowding my space on the River Walk. Time to go. Forget the package. I walked back to the motel, got Steve up to shower, and loaded the car, mumbling to myself about the delay.

For, perhaps the fiftieth time on this trip I repacked the overnight bags, food items, computer bags, camera bags, laundry, maps, travel books, notebooks, and finally my butt-pack that kept my money, lip gloss, and aspirin close at hand. There were times on the trip I sat frustrated, thinking I needed something I left at home only to realize that I had it—in the car. It was a realization that made me smile every time. Everything we physically needed was in that car. For a moment, I thought I could live like that. I could travel the country forever.

I went back into the room to do a last check to make sure I had all the bags. A picture of a collared peccary lay on the nightstand.

"Hey Steve, what's this?"

"It's a picture of a peccary that was sitting on a rock outside the Alamo. It was folded into a Moravian star. Remember when we did those? I thought it was cool, so I kept it. It means we will soon see a real peccary. It's called serendipity. The lady in the office told me about that. She said it was serendipity that she met me."

"Really? Humm. That's interesting. What did she mean?"

"I don't know."

"You didn't ask?"

Steve came out to the car, showered and even more cheerful than usual. As I was putting the finishing touches on the re-packing, he grabbed for the bag of cookies from the food cooler.

"Hey, not cookies. We're going to lunch in ten minutes. Here, have a few crackers."

"You don't eat crackers in the bed of your future!"

It was a line from *The Tick*. I giggled, and he loved that I did and grabbed the crackers and a juice box drink. When we finally got on the road, I told him it would be a long day of driving.

"I would like to make it to Carlsbad tonight and we're leaving late so I won't be stopping much. Can you take it?"

He replied with another Tick quote, "Whatever you say but prepare yourself for swift justice."

I giggled again.

Steve put on his headphones. I put on an Eagles CD and spent several hours driving in quiet contemplation.

The drive from San Antonio to Fort Stockton is long, straight, and boring—300 miles of western scrub brush and tumbleweeds with few signs of life except for the road-kill skunks and circling turkey vultures. I swept by Sonora and Ozona, barely recognizing their existence, finally getting into Fort Stockton around dinner time. I was still alert from a shot of afternoon caffeine, so we stopped to eat at a steak house and then drove a couple more hours into Carlsbad. The night air was invigorating. It was mostly the humidity that dropped, but it was finally comfortable outside. We rolled down the windows and stuck our arms out and at the Motel 6 in Carlsbad I left the door open until bedtime just to get a taste of unconditioned air for the first time in two months. The next morning, we were on our way to Carlsbad Caverns.

Most of us have few memories of our very young childhood. Perhaps that's a good thing overall, but I have a distinct memory of the time I got bit by a dog. I mentioned it to my mother years ago, saying it was the reason I was afraid of dogs.

My mother gasped and said, "You were only sixteen months old. You can't remember that!"

"Well, do we have a picture of it?"

"Of course not."

"Then, I remember it. It was a big fluffy white dog that I now recognize as a collie, and I went over to hug him. I can see his face right now. I can see how he was laying at the bottom of the steps. As I moved in to hug him, he bit me on the face across my eye. But it begs the question Mom, if I was so young, why was I left to wander the trailer park alone?"

I was only half-joking. I really wanted to know.

She gave me a scowl and snapped, "People looked out for each other back then."

"Apparently not."

There are a few other early memory snippets. I remember having whooping cough at the same time as my little brother while at some cheap motel in North Dakota on the way to a church convention. I remember that we sat in bed all night throwing up and wheezing. I remember being scared.

I remember seeing my father feed a standing grizzly bear in Yellowstone.

And I remember seeing a giant hole in the earth they called Carlsbad Caverns. I wondered if I would remember it as big as it seemed to be then.

"Hey Steve. When we get inside, you need to stay with me and not go running ahead. It's dark in there and I won't be going as fast as you."

No answer.

"Steve, you're staying with me, right?"

"Yes, yes. I won't run off. Sometimes you make my head hurt, Pinky."

From the cave's natural entrance, it's about a three-hour,

self-guided walk. It was a decent workout—about two-and-a-half miles, some of it steep as you descend 750 feet down a dimly lit path into our ancient past.

It is hard to grasp the sense of things far away in space—but inside a cavern the world is enormous; the earth is turned inside out exposing evolving mineral forms, giant limestone, and gypsum crystals that take familiar shapes. Most already have names, Totem Pole, Witch's Finger, Giant Dome, Bottomless Pit, Fairyland, or the Doll's Theater.

Steve started pointing some of them out and creating a story to go with them.

"Mom, look at that one. An old man was frozen in a crystalline mass, one leg raised in flight, his face paralyzed in a state of fear as he tried to escape but got caught in an alien mineral flow. His image is now permanently etched into the cave."

He continued, "And that one over there looks like you. It's a mom in a long flowing dress leaning over to a little kid and pointing her finger. She's mad because he just made that mess on the floor."

"What? I don't do that."

Anyone Out There?

Southwestern New Mexico

An occasional windmill was evidence someone was out there living in near desolation without a shade tree, edible vegetation, or a body of water for fifty miles. When you finally see a house, it's usually a converted trailer surrounded by a dozen old cars, scattered machine parts, propane tanks, a rusted broken-down tractor, and the biggest satellite dish you've ever seen. These are the people that will survive earth's future meltdown. Those and of course a couple hundred thousand crazy politicians, arrogant socialites, toxic celebs, and Bilderberg families who have invitations to Fed-sponsored underground bunkers. That's the future of the human race— the worst of the worst will survive.

As desolate as it seems, there is a feeling that something is going on. You can sense it. Barbed-wire fences, gated roads that seem to go nowhere on the map. Government ops underground. Airstrips tucked in between mountains. But we didn't go looking for secret government facilities. We were on another mission. Gem hunting. Beneath the rippling red rock mesas and the quiet grasses waving in a slow breeze are stones people spend lifetimes hunting down, digging up, and trying to sell for a few dollars.

Cheryl, the gospel-singing geologist we met in Panama City Beach told us about gem hunting in New Mexico, and we wanted to do real gem hunting, not the stocked tourist-mines where you pay $20 for a sieve, pale and stocked stream. So, I stopped at a hardware store for two rock hammers and buckets. Next, a stop at a bookstore for *Gem Hunting in New Mexico*.

Steve and I poured over the maps and decided on several spots in the direction we were headed, Lordsburg to Luna with a lunchtime pit stop at some ghost town in between. We were both excited to take the Blazer off-road again, and I had come prepared with a couple of planks of wood in case we got stuck in mud or sand somewhere off the main road. It was not likely there would be mud. It was dry and hot and looked like it had been for weeks, maybe months. Off-road was mostly large gravel paths partially covered by low scrub with the occasional beer bottles off to the side. We drove about twenty miles down two gravel roads, following the markers in the book. I stopped the Blazer somewhere past Lordsburg. We collected our gear and packed some water, even though we would not stray far from the car.

"Okay, Steve. We stay in sight of each other and stick to the gullies. And remember, keep your socks pulled up and over your pant legs and use the stick to poke around the rocks. Snakes, scorpions. You know."

As always, I repeated myself with him and waited until I got a response. "Scorpions and snakes. Did you hear me?"

Was he listening? Steve's mind was always in multiple places at once—but then, so was mine.

"Meat! You worry too much! I gotcha. I'll poke with the stick."

I smiled and moved away from him and into a shallow gully. I poked at a smallish gray rock, thinking it looked promising. Cheryl told us that the plainest rocks on the outside can have the most exceptional interior.

I glanced up to survey our position. It was so quiet I could hear the air swirling in my ears. Steve was crouched down about twenty feet away, putting a couple of rocks in his bucket, and brushing something off his leg. *Relax, I whispered to myself. I brought a snakebite kit. Yeah, like I've ever used one. What's that poem? Red and gold kills a... Red and black is safe or... something.* Whatever. The only snake I would recognize would be a rattler.

"Ants," he called out, seeing the concern on my face.

In the many times we poked around in rocks and rubble in the middle of nowhere, we never saw a snake or any signs of life except lizards and ants.

We continued pushing around the rocks in the gully, brushing aside bits of vegetation and gravel, picking certain stones up for close-up inspection. We were looking for rocks that were different—anything out of the ordinary—too rough, too smooth, very round or oddly shaped. We wanted the ones that stood out. Like people, I thought. Those would be the most interesting.

After a couple of hours, it was nearly noon. We went back to the car and poured out the bucket contents onto a towel. We examined the pictures in the book and optimistically believed we found several varieties of jasper, agate, desert rose, smoky quartz, and opal. Whatever we had, we had two buckets of it. We stayed in Lordsburg for the night and would do more gem hunting the next day. It's easy to get hooked; something like gambling. You always think the big one is just ahead.

Besides gem hunting, I heard there were a few ghost towns in New Mexico. At a gift-store gas stop, I asked a few locals what they recommended. Most gave me strange looks. I got the feeling that what I considered to be a ghost town was, by New Mexico standards, just a regular town with some older-than-usual buildings.

A man standing next to me at the counter said, "Go to MUG-ee-un. It's not far north up 180, at 159, I think. You'll see a sign."

Back in the car, I looked for it on the map. There was nothing that resembled *Mugeeun* on the map, but on our way to Luna on our second day of gem-hunting, I saw a sign at crossroad 159. It said Mogollon, and I assumed that was it. I discovered later that Mogollon is pronounced *Mugeeun.*

Highway 180 runs between the San Francisco Ridge and the Mogollon Mountains in southwestern New Mexico. A historical marker designates road 159, also known as Bursum

Road, as the way up to the town. There were no warnings about the road other than the requirement for chains in the winter. I don't know if it would have deterred me to know that it was nine miles along a steep, roughly paved winding, and narrow one-lane road or that it ascends 2,000 feet in seven miles or that none of the hairpin turn-backs have guardrails. But I didn't know as I turned onto the road up to Mogollon. About a quarter of the way up, I got nervous as the road began to snake upward and narrowed to one lane. There were spectacular glimpses off the ridge if you dared to look. The cliff was getting steeper and an occasional truck (only saw one) coming down the mountain toward us was a scary event—the truck pulled over with wheels nearly off the steep edge, allowing us to pass. There was no turning back—I couldn't turn around on the road, and I certainly couldn't back down.

Steve was sitting straight up in his seat. I was gripping the wheel and breathing deep. There was no choice. I just took it slow and continued up the road around a number of hairpin turns. None had guardrails; not sure that would have mattered. I would not have wanted to do that drive without a four-wheel-drive vehicle, but that wasn't on the sign below. We both took a breath when the town came into view. I was already wondering if there was another road out.

There were maybe two dozen old buildings in need of a lot of repairs, including a theater, saloon, and general store. Several buildings had For Sale signs. Everything seemed deserted, but people were there somewhere, evidenced by the hanging plant and wind chimes on one porch. There was no place to stay or eat. We saw no one, but there were muffled voices in the hills and the sounds of chisels and hammers tapping rocks and a few old cars.

"Want to take a hike up the road and see what's up there?"

He nodded. "This place is kind of cool. What's that sound in the hills?"

"Miners or gem hunters like us only a lot more organized and knowledgeable about rocks. The people up here are serious. That's how they make their living. I can't imagine it would be much."

"Do they live here, too? There're no stores or anything."

"I have no idea. There are a few cars over there so, maybe."

We walked up Bursum Road and found Fannie Road with more old and abandoned buildings. Still, no person, dog, or squirrel anywhere to be seen. After a mile, we ran into the Mogollon Cemetery and wandered around trying not to step on any graves, although many were covered in brush and overgrown grass. The gravesites appeared to be scattered about randomly. The oldest we saw was 1874. Some had gates and a fence still standing, but in poor repair.

Around one of the larger fenced gravesites, four large logs had either fallen or been pushed into a circle near each other to accommodate a seating arrangement. I called Steve to sit and have lunch.

"It's weird being here," he said. "Did you notice that there were a lot of deaths in 1918?"

"No, I didn't. That's interesting. Maybe there was a mining accident or something. I was looking at ages, curious at the number of young ones that died."

I handed Steve a cheese sandwich, and that's when I saw them. "Steve. Look."

Three collared peccaries were rooting around one of the trees about fifteen yards away.

"Collared peccaries!" he whispered. "I knew we would see one. We should be quiet. They can be mean."

I didn't like the looks of them, and there was a baby in the group. They were bigger than I thought.

I whispered, "Yeah. Can we go?"

A half-hour later we were back on 159 but heading the other way out of town. It turned out to be much longer and still steep and winding, but not nearly as scary as the drive up to Mogollon.

One of our gem-hunting expeditions took us through a town called Luna where we discovered the 'Luna one-finger-wave'. Everyone that passed us in their car, whether we were in the car or rock hunting near the road, gave us the one-finger-wave—a simple raise of the pointer finger from the hand on the steering wheel. After a couple of times, Steve and I thought they were trying to tell us something, so we stopped and inspected the car. But on the next occurrence of the wave, we weren't in the car; we were gem-poking roadside. I thought maybe we looked like locals to them—that we were being mistaken for people they knew. I decided that wasn't likely. A blonde mom and son carrying buckets and digging in the dry riverbed just off the road near a brand-new Blazer with bikes on the back? I don't think we could have been mistaken for locals.

Steve understood before I did, "Mom, they're waving to us."

Finally, we clued in and waved back.

Continuing north and west, we passed through Alpine, Arizona looking for a place to stay for the night. We passed on the Tall Wi Wi Lodge but not without a good laugh. We were looking for the usual Sportsman's Lodge and Cattleman's Steakhouse, which seemed to be in every small southwestern town, but found their cousins, the Springerville Inn and Booger Red's Cafe.

Booger Red's had exactly what we were craving. Steve ordered a cheese sandwich with as many cheese types as they had, and I asked for the pork chops and mashed potatoes. I ordered them my usual way.

"I'll have the pork chops and burn 'em," I said to a beautiful young waitress with long flowing brown hair, soft brown eyes, and a milky complexion.

I suddenly pictured her in five years, raising a herd of kids, bringing her cowboy husband a beer in front of the television, and growing a hundred fat cells for every pair of dirty boxers she took to the laundromat. *How cynical and judgmental of me. I need to stop that. Maybe he'll turn out to be the Man From Snowy River.*

I guess she had never heard the term 'burn 'em' as it applied to meat. Most just laugh and say 'no problem' knowing I meant very well done. But the brown-eyed girl took me seriously. After thirty minutes waiting for our dinner, she brought the food and apologized for not being able to get the chops any darker or, she worried, it would take even longer.

I looked down at the blackish pork chop chips and smiled. She didn't understand 'burn 'em' and we didn't understand the one-finger-wave. A semantic gap, but a tasty end to our romp through New Mexico.

Road Noise

Boys will be Boys

Durango, Colorado

Anyone who took a Women's Studies course before the end of the millennium was told that gender is a social construct—that we, and the Village, train girls from the start to be nice, quiet, social, and natural-mommies by dressing them in pink, giving them dolls and allowing them to be bad at math. Similarly, boys are natural-born thugs because we teach them to be tough. Nature versus nurture.

I took that seriously. I wanted to raise a kinder, gentler male. So, in 1983, when my son was born, his first toy was a doll. Actually, two Cabbage Patch dolls. They were boy dolls—Errol and Freddie—I thought he might identify with them more if they were dressed as boys would be. Every morning I would find the dolls undressed and thrown outside the crib. He didn't like them, he didn't play with them, and he didn't want them occupying crib space. That was true for any stuffed animal in his crib except for the stuffed airplane that played *Fly Me to the Moon*. For whatever reason he allowed the airplane to stay in the crib even though he couldn't wind it up himself but would hold it up to me and say, "wine dup."

Despite my attempts at making Steve a kinder, gentler male through the provision of softer, nicer toys, his favorite toy was a $1.99 space shuttle with wind-up wheels that made noise when pushed along the floor. In fact, anything that made lots of noise and had wheels was good. He loved insects, getting dirty, never got cold, and would occasionally pee in the yard (even though, to my knowledge, he never saw anyone do that). And, by the way, pushing the dolls on him and making him wear cute socks that I bought in the girls' department, did not make him gay.

Boys will be boys. Do you know that boys set plastic action figures on fire, jump out of second-story windows onto trampolines (!!No!!), and throw dead monitors off the top floor of high-rise parking garages?

The great thing about boys is that you know where you stand. They will beat each other up one minute and be playing together the next. They say it like it is—and it doesn't change when they get older. "Dude, you really smell, man." Girls will hold a grudge for years, play coy and innocent, make up stories about you, stab you in the back, not let you into their sororities for unknown reasons, and then years later at a reunion pretend they were your friends. Maybe that was just me.

Boys are unique creatures. They prefer gross humor, wildlife that oozes slime, and they have little dedication to personal appearance. Boys also help each other with no expectations—no hidden agenda. They have a hierarchy that is accepted and observed. You don't interfere with that by demanding they play nice. Unless they are about to kill each other—you let it unfold. There will be people who disagree with me, but they probably don't have boys. And yes, that applies to some girls too. You can try to make them sit and conform—but I think it better to corral them and channel the energy, if possible. Good luck with that. The problem is—corralling that energy is extraordinarily time-consuming and exhausting to the point of collapse, particularly for a single mother with a job. That is why moms reach for the wine at dinner time, buy boys the blood-and-guts video games, and let them eat dinner in front of the television.

Throughout this trip Steve had been far more interested in roadside smells, identifying roadkill, the endless search for lizards and other small slimy wildlife, and stopping at go-kart tracks. He tolerated the Bridges of Madison County (that was only because there were bats in the rafters) and the San Antonio River Walk (which is really just a pretty walk along the river, so hard to blame him for that), he liked *Phantom of the Opera* on Broadway (probably because it is such a visual show), seemed interested in the MoMA and tolerated The Met.

Now we were in Durango, Colorado and I thought, *horses*. We'll horseback ride in the Rockies! We'll both love that. And we did, and probably for different reasons. I found Rapp Corral, and we lucked out as the riding group comprised three other boys about Steve's age. They all hit it off immediately. With an excellent female guide, we took off for a four-hour ride through the birch trees and along the cliff tops of the San Juan Mountains overlooking the Animas River Valley above

Durango. At times, the trail seemed steep to me, and I wondered if the horse sensed my fear. I tried to fake confidence, but whatever the horse knew about me it continued sure-footed down the path, unconcerned. The boys seemed naturally confident with the horses—even Steve, who, except for the pony-picture-taking event at his daycare center in Carmel, California, had never been on a horse before.

As suspected, the boys laughed repeatedly about the horses' various bodily noises, droppings, and smells. The guide and I caught each other's eye now and then and just let it be. The youngest of the boys (lowest on the male hierarchy in this tribe) was constantly chastised by the others for talking too much, yet they were all there at the rest stop to lend the little guy a hand off his horse and guide him to the lizard locating and poking area designated by the elder tribesmen.

At one stop, we left the horses and hiked to a cave in the side of the hill. We hiked to the end, about twenty yards, and with flashlights provided by the guide, searched for bats and salamanders and even turned the lights out for a minute. Even the boys were quiet.

It turned out to be a glorious morning, sunny, warm, and peaceful. I noted the contrasts between mountains and green valleys, white birch trees and purple wildflowers, nature, and our boys. It would be such a crime to take that nature out of them.

I got to thinking about the day. Boys. Horses. They're a lot alike. Horses respond to the subtlest cues—cues that most riders don't even notice. Like mothers or parents, tuning-in is so critical and yet so easy to overlook. It's easier to focus on technique or outcomes that stare you in the eye. Boys, like horses, respond to consistency, predictability, and sometimes letting them run free. We don't need to *fix* boys and make them more like girls.

Later that night at the motel, I watched him reading his *Guide to Western Reptiles and Amphibians,* and I couldn't help myself. I went over and sat on his bed and fussed with his hair and asked about his favorite part of the book. He quickly flipped to the page with a green tree frog.

"I've seen tons of these guys. Can I get a frog when we get home?"

How could I refuse?

Road Noise

Spirit in the Sky

Mesa Verde to Grand Junction, Colorado

Dark clouds were gathering as we left Durango for Mesa Verde. It was 9 AM and, aside from the chafing on my inner thighs from the previous day's horseback ride, I was bouncing with energy. The air was alive. Perhaps with the Great Spirit of the Hopi.

The Four Corners is the only place in the US where four states (Arizona, New Mexico, Utah, and Colorado) come together. According to the Great Spirit, the area is sacred and a microcosm of the entire planet. Violations of nature in the Mesa Verde/Four Corners region will be echoed across the Earth—violations like the uranium stripped from the ground in the area that created weapons of war. According to Hopi and other believers, the Four Corners area is a source of positive and negative ions in the atmosphere—a vortex where the energy current must be kept in balance to maintain life on planet Earth as we wait for the coming Fifth Age of Man.

"The time for the lone wolf is over. Gather yourselves!
Banish the word struggle from your attitude and your

vocabulary. All that we do now must be done in a sacred manner and in celebration."
---Hopi Elders' Prophecy

Whether by Hopi prophecy or the brewing thunderstorm's electrical charge, there was a palpable energy in the air. We were ready to climb into the spirit of the Anasazi, ascend the rock walls to the ancestors of the Hopi, and get a sense of these people of the land.

Getting to Mesa Verde took longer than expected. It was a long drive to the cliffs and once you get there, there is a lot to see. You can take self-guided walks to several ruins and spend hours exploring the area. There are over 600 cliff dwellings, and a few can be seen up close with a guided tour. We started with guided tours of Cliff Palace and Balcony House, and then a self-guided tour of Spruce Tree House.

Cliff Palace is the largest cliff dwelling in the park. Getting in and out of Cliff Palace is challenging but fun as the trail takes you up steep ladders and sandstone stairs that have been cut into narrow cracks between the boulders.

Balcony House, while smaller than Cliff Palace, is a more intimate look at the civilization that lived there, but to get to the site you must first descend a stairway path about ninety feet toward the site, then up a three-story wooden ladder that hung on the cliff below the alcove ruins, crawl through a tight tunnel, and then climb sixty feet straight up on ladders and more stone steps. Strenuous but fun except for the lightning. One of the rangers even remarked about a woman being struck the prior year which no one seemed thrilled to hear.

Thunderstorms, lightning, rain, and mist followed us much of the day, but we took our chances and kept on climbing, taking moments to glance out at the valley floor and the dark purple sky that surrounded us. Green mesas (Mesa Verde), steep rock cliffs diving into the earth, dark skies with flashing daggers striking the earth, electrical charge in the air, negative ions swirling in your blood—how easy it is to feel the energy of the Four Corners and the Great Spirit in the sky.

Our guide was a Hopi Indian who took a great deal of time speculating on the lifestyle, daily rituals, ceremonies, and possibilities related to the abrupt disappearance of the cliff dwellers—alien abduction, not ruled out. I would like to have heard a bit about the geology of the rock and the composition and mechanics of building the structures, but he had his focus, and it was interesting to hear.

The rain started again as we stood inside Balcony House, several thousand feet above the valley below. I stood there looking out over the sea of rock cliffs, the rain mist hitting my face, and tried to feel what it would have been like a thousand years ago. For that moment, I wished I could have been alone, standing there among the history and spirit in the rocks. It was easy to feel the energy and electrical charge in the air, and I noticed a few of the other visitors moving to quiet areas to contemplate the ancients. Most of the tourists seemed oblivious to the energy—busying themselves with details of the kivas or characteristics of the stone. But not Steve. He had noticed.

"Hey, Mom. Do you think they ever just sat here near the edge and just stared out at the sky? We're so high up. Maybe that's why they built stuff here."

"I think you're right. Maybe the cliff dwellers came here not just to hide from competing clans or escape the elements but because they wanted to be alone, up here in the clouds, touching the sky, with eagles and hawks. I would."

We heard the guide's voice. Steve and I wandered back to the group that was standing around a kiva opening—a hole in the ground where ceremonies took place. I looked around at the group.

There were no children other than Steve and no single parents, as was the case this entire trip. There were several middle-aged and retired couples, two young couples, and an Eastern European group of six adults.

The experience of Mesa Verde lifted my spirits. The rain was cleansing and energizing so, even though it was early afternoon, we got back in the car and headed north up Highway 550 toward Ouray and ultimately for Utah.

The highway was steep in places and winding throughout, so it took longer than expected. We stopped at many of the overlooks so I could get a break from driving and get a look at the scenery. Misty clouds clung to purple mountains rising over oceanic expanses of deep green forests. As my friend had insisted, it was one of the most beautiful routes on our trip, a postcard stereotype of the rugged west. People in covered wagons crossed these mountains. I can't even imagine. No wonder many died trying.

We stopped in Ouray for an early dinner before continuing toward Utah. It was getting late in the day and the gray skies were making it darker. The towns after Ouray are too small or scarce for motels and it was getting too late to camp, so I kept driving. Steve was on the computer with headphones, and I was trying to focus on the roads to be careful not to miss a turnoff. I had taken some backroads thinking I could cut over to Utah, but quickly decided that was a bad idea. I knew there must be some backroads that went west all the way over to Moab. As the crow flies, we weren't that far away—but it was getting near dark. Some sort of sense took over, and the thought of getting lost or stranded out there on some gravel road for even a night brought visions of the man-with-the-hook or bigfoot or perhaps just cold, wet, and sleeping upright in the car again.

So, after briefly getting lost and shuffling around a few backroads, I pulled back on to 550 and took the sensible way to Grand Junction, where we spent the night.

Road Noise

Red Rocks and Hard Bodies

Moab, Utah

Red dust swirled up in front of the car as the tires spun to a stop in front of the Lazy Lizard Hostel in Moab, Utah. Coffee and a sunrise start out of Grand Junction got us into the red planet in less than two hours.

A tap on Steve's headphones brought him out from under while I was already scrambling out of the car. A call ahead a few days ago had confirmed that we had the last couple of bunk beds in all of Moab. It was Labor Day week and the RVs, ATVs, and 4WDs pulling assorted hike, bike, sail, and raft gear had descended on little Moab. A glance around confirmed. Hell yes. I was surrounded by young tight men in snug shorts and sweaty tees.

I was still checking out the scenery when Steve passed me carrying our overnight bags, the camera bag, and my bottle of distilled water. Finally. Seventy-some-days into our ninety-day adventure and he finally grabbed the bags without me asking. What a long, strange learning curve it's been.

I went inside to check in. Several people were ahead of us.

A twenty-something young man waved me ahead of him. As he moved, sunlight from the window lit up part of his face and tousled blonde hair like a picture on the cover of a romance novel. I continued with that thought. He was wearing torn jeans and a long sleeve white shirt with rolled cuffs and silver embroidery that curved from his shoulders down the open neckline toward his waist. Only one button held the shirt snug to his sides, and a single white stone hung around his neck from a black cord.

"I'm just waiting for a friend. It's cool." He smiled, winked at me, and nodded at Steve. "Hey dude. Where are you guys from?"

I gave him the short version of the three-month trip story before stepping up to the counter to check in. I almost regretted the quick service.

"Sounds like an awesome trip. Well, hey, you guys take care. You'll like Moab. My buddy and I have been here for a week and we're getting ready to leave—back to Bend. My last year at OSU."

Oh my god, he was like—twenty-one.

I turned toward the manager. He was equally young and cute. Maybe it was just me.

"You guys are in the co-ed dorm room, you know. Sorry, but that's all we have. It will be fine. Everybody is cool here and most people sack out by 11. A lot of people haven't checked in yet, so you should have your pick of beds."

I had no problem sharing a dorm room with a bunch of young guys (and probably some girls, too). We picked two beds in a far corner and geared up for some hiking and lizard hunting. The Arches today, Canyonlands tomorrow.

Arches is a red desert containing the world's largest assortment of natural sandstone monuments. It's remote and dry and its grandest inhabitants are the alien creature-shaped and eroded rock that is perpetually changed by the elements and will, one day, erode away. They form arches, people-shaped spires, X-rated pinnacles, and rock towers in Zen-like balance—a red-rock Rorschach. See what you want to see—women in long dresses, kings in tall hats, giant rabbits, or phallic body parts. Let's be clear about this; there are penis-shaped rocks everywhere in Arches National Park. Even a six-year-old would notice. A kid of about that age passing us in the other direction on the trail said, "… but Daddy, it looked like a penis." I am guessing Daddy was trying to divert his son's curiosity about the rock shapes, but nature frequently claims sexual shapes—usually in more subtle forms. The forms at Arches are not subtle.

We took the hike to Delicate Arch, which you can't see from the road that winds through the park. Up close it towers above smooth-looking but sandpapery slick-rock canyons. The hike is easy, but if you're a kid or want to work on those leg muscles, you can take a few of the steeper ways up to the arch. I took the easy way. Steve scrambled up a steeper side-route. I was glad I insisted we carry extra water and food. It was hot. There were lots of people and no shade unless you were under a foot tall.

We were covered in red dust when we got back to the car but brushed off and drove on to the next arch group that included the Double Arch and Balanced Rock. More hiking. More red dust. Fewer people as the heat rose and families were taking little ones back to town for air-conditioned fast-food and hotels with swimming pools. We didn't mind the heat. We shared a granola bar, a bottle of water to drink, and another to pour over our heads.

The next day, we drove a little further south to the Canyonlands, another inverse mountain range carved by the Colorado and Green River. The alien landscape continued with multicolored sandstone cliffs, ribbon-like gorges, and imposing views from sheer cliff tops and if you know where to look, you can find the petroglyphs, evidence of the ancient civilizations that lived there. We didn't find them.

We hiked the ridge tops of the Canyon, a smaller version of the Grand Canyon without the hotels, gift shops, tour guides, buses, helicopters, hordes of people, and gas stations and it is that very remoteness that makes it so inviting, peaceful and special.

Steve found lizards in every crevice, which he gently picked up, petted, microscopically observed eyeball-to-eyeball, and then laid back into a crack of their great stone fortress. Life was evident only in the sparse brushy plants that had managed to push through the rock to the surface and in the small brown lizards that have adapted by eating the same plants that shelter them.

We got back in the car and took a few backroads along the top of the Canyon, stopping a few more times at vast overlooks or interesting rock formations. There were few people on the road and even fewer the more we hiked in. I was cautious not to go too far with no one else around. Hawks flew overhead and nested in the ridges of the cliffs and seemed oblivious to our presence. It was so quiet you could only hear the weight of the air on your eardrums.

Back at the hostel, I cleaned up with a shower. When I came downstairs to make us some dinner, I found Steve talking to three twenty-something girls from Switzerland. They were all sitting at the base of the stairway between the kitchen and living areas, which were bustling with activity.

"Is this your son? He's so funny and sweet. What an old soul." Those were comments I heard often about Steve.

He was examining the Swiss coins they had given him. He had developed a knack for charming foreign money from the ladies. First, he would tell them about our trip and then bring out the show-and-tell—starting with his frog box we bought at the Tampa aquarium that housed his collection of foreign coins, then his collection of cheesy key chains from gas-station-gift shops across the country and if that didn't wow them, he brought out the silk brown lizard and the fish fossil, proving a funny story to go with each. That was usually enough to get the ladies giggling and handing over foreign coins to add to his collection.

As he continued to socialize, I made dinner—some leftover

chicken, dense country bread we bought at a Durango bakery, and fresh raw cauliflower.

I took the paper plate out to him and said, "I have a treat, too." I produced a bottle of chocolate milk and the bag of dill pickle chips I had stashed away a few weeks ago. After we left the east coast, we never saw dill pickle chips again.

"Awesome, Mom!"

"Share them with your friends and then come up to shower and bed soon, okay? And say your goodbyes because we're leaving early tomorrow."

"Yes, master." He was already opening the bag of chips.

"Eat the other stuff first," I called over my shoulder as I continued up the stairs.

"Ah, yes," he said. "And then we will celebrate the occasion with the adding of chocolate to milk."

I heard the girls' giggle. I wonder if they knew that was a line from Homer Simpson.

I got in bed and took out my notebook and pen while I waited for Steve. I knew I wouldn't be able to go to sleep until he was in the bunk above me.

The handsome young man in the bed across from me asked if I was keeping a journal. He must have been about twenty-five and was partially upright, leaning on his elbow. A tank shirt revealed his muscular shoulders, and he had on maroon boxers as he stretched out on the bed without a blanket or sheet. I never asked him his name, and he didn't ask mine, but we talked for a while without the burden of small talk. I talked about my travels across the US and the hostels where we had stayed. I recommended a few to him. He was from Belgium, with a charming French accent, traveling alone for the summer. He was just out of college and was traveling the Southwest before joining the working world.

Steve came in with still-damp hair from his shower. He jumped into the top bunk violently shaking both our beds. He wanted to talk, and he tried, but his voice trailed off and he was asleep in two minutes.

I said goodnight to the boy in the bunk above—and the boy from Belgium.

Road Noise

Broken and Closed

Blanding, Utah

After two days hiking and hanging around buffed young men in shorts and sweaty T-shirts, I needed some downtime— an evening watching motel television with Steve after a steak dinner and a couple of Dewar's neat would do it.

We were headed for the Grand Canyon. The nearest town in-between big enough for a motel was Blanding near Natural Bridges National Monument. The motel advertised a hot tub. Despite the daytime heat, the evenings were cooling just enough, and a hot tub sounded good. I was beginning to feel the strain of all the hiking and horseback riding, from which I had acquired some frightening-looking black and blue areas on my inner thighs.

The outside was not much to see. They never are. As we walked in, I noticed the office was also the laundry room, storage closet, and library. The family, which included a daughter who looked to be about sixteen, were all gathered in the room and performing various chores. The girl folded laundry, the woman entered numbers into a large record book (not a computer) and the man walked gingerly over to me. He was at least seven feet tall with teeth that stuck straight out in the front. I wondered how he could eat.

"I see you have a hot tub?"

"Actually, it's broken at the moment. We're wait'n on a part. Should be here next week." He responded as if he thought I still might be there next week.

"How much is a room?" I sighed.

While I stood there, the tall man and the woman, I assumed was his wife although she appeared significantly younger, discussed the room price and whether it had just changed to the lower winter rate. I pointed out that since the hot tub wasn't working and they had advertised it, perhaps the winter rate would be appropriate, anyway. They reluctantly agreed to the $5 discount.

After checking-in and unloading a few bags, it seemed there was also no phone in the room, the ice machine in the hall didn't work, the sink squirted water out of the sides instead of the bottom, and to top it off, the tub-shower combo had permanent reddish-brown stains that covered most of the bottom of the tub. It crossed my mind that maybe someone had died there. That thought slipped away as I went to do a bed check. I did my usual mattress check for bugs, put the bedspreads face down on the carpet, and brought in the sleeping bags and pillows from the car. The whole thing hardly fazed me anymore. Steve didn't notice any of it. Hadn't the entire trip—nearly ten weeks.

I was getting used to cheap motel accommodations, but

what bothered me was the fluctuating rates. Independently owned motels often had rates that seem to have a distinct relationship to the looks and home-origin of the potential clientele. I noticed more than one motel manager give a slight hesitation and a quick glance toward my car before giving me a room rate while mumbling something about summer rates or weekend rates or you-look-like-you're-from-California rates. They often glanced down after the rate quote avoiding my eyes. Guilt for overcharging me? What could I do? Argue? Who would I complain to? This was one of those towns, and one of those motels. It only existed as a place in-between.

When I asked the manager about the lack of a phone in the room, he mumbled again through those pointed teeth, that there was a public phone at the gas station a half-mile away.

"Maybe you could have mentioned this before I checked in? Look, it wouldn't be a problem except my cell phone isn't working. Is there no cell service here either?"

"Our cell tower's been down—struck by lightning last week, but it's about a hundred miles from here and we don't get much service anyway."

So, I was without communication and a hot tub. All right then—a steak dinner and some scotch, and at least the television worked.

It was a Friday night around 6 PM. The streets seemed nearly deserted. Restaurants seemed closed. After searching for a market that was open, it occurred to me that we were in Mormon country. After a cruise of the only main street in town, I found one place open, and the sign said it was a bar and restaurant. Finally. Civilization.

We walked in and were the only people there. The place looked more like a craft store that served food. There were cutesy hats and teddy bears on shelves and the back of booths, embroidered plaques with inspirational sayings all over the walls, old baskets of dusty dried flowers—dust collectors everywhere. But there was a beautiful mahogany liquor bar that stood on one side of the room. The mirror behind the bar was etched glass, but there were no shelves in front. I inquired about it since I did not see any bottles of liquor, but I thought maybe they served wine. The waitress gave me a quick laugh instead and confirmed that it used to be a liquor bar but was now an ice cream bar.

I was annoyed now, "You know your sign says restaurant AND bar."

"It is a bar, just an ice cream one."

Her voice was sugary-sweet with a distinctly judgmental and condescending tone.

Ah yes. Blind trust of the church (any organized religion—no need to single out Mormons), superior attitude, twisted logic, thinking you know the answers to the great mysteries of life without ever picking up a book that isn't handed to you by the church. Archaic laws that make no sense, follow the rules, ignore inconsistencies—there must be a reason—we just don't know what that might be. I said this to myself, of course, because I believe anyone can believe anything they want to believe. Aliens? Fine. Cruel god? Okay. Whatever.

I returned a sarcastic smile toward her and noticed her super-soft rounded features without a hint of a wrinkle. She couldn't have been over eighteen.

"Fine. We'll have two chicken dinners with mashed potatoes and gravy. Please put our gravy on the side."

Steve picked up on my tone. *Yes, I suppose I had a tone.*

I clarified with the annoyance still in my voice, "It must be a dry town. Dry means no alcohol. It's a Mormon religious thing. But you can eat chocolate cake until you drop dead from diabetes or in this case (as I checked the menu), marionberry pie and ice cream. Let's get some to go and eat it 'till we're sick, okay?"

His eyebrow raised. He caught my sarcasm and disapproved. "People can believe what they want, you know."

"Absolutely."

I taught him that.

Road Noise

Small Footprints

Grand Canyon, Arizona

The colors of the southern Utah-Arizona border were coming into focus. Red monuments surrounded by rusted barbed-wire fences. They were there to keep tourists out.

Monument Valley is owned and operated by the Navajo Nation, the largest reservation in the United States. There was only one main road near Monument Valley, US 163, which runs along the southeast side. Signs were few and vague and the area itself provided no tourist information. You got the distinct feeling the Navajos did not want your presence on their land. But they wanted your money. What a dilemma. You can pay $5 to drive the 17-mile loop, but the most spectacular areas of Monument Valley, like the ruins, petroglyphs, and arches, are accessible only with a paid Navajo guide. I don't blame them; unsupervised visitors tend to leave large footprints and candy wrappers.

There's about a hundred miles of empty road between Blanding, Utah, and the border of Arizona at the red edge of Monument Valley. Every few miles a string of weathered umbrella covered shelters with small wooden tables dotted the highway selling local jewelry and crafts at inflated prices. On down the road were big-market Teepee stores selling more of the same at even higher prices.

I wasn't surprised at the overpricing, but I was by the attitude encountered in the Teepee stores. I stopped at three and at every one I got attitude—ignored, a nasty look or a zombie-like greeting. There was never a welcome and never a thank you. I didn't stop at another one. But at the next three roadside tables, I bought silver earrings, a turquoise bracelet, and Steve bought a bag of colorful rocks. In return, I got smiles and a thank you.

The drive continued through undeveloped or deserted land where skinny cattle and horses roamed outside of gates grazing just off the roadside. Run-down trailers with wooden or cloth lean-to awnings clustered in small groups on the horizon of the barren landscape. Graveyards of rusted and hollow car bodies and unrecognizable scraps of metal sat just outside the weathered trailers and shacks.

Steve and I had been anxiously awaiting our time in the Grand Canyon. We arrived at the Canyon early. I had a reservation at Mather Campground on the South Rim. Mather is near the village and activity center, which was ideal for us since it was our first time there and we didn't know our way around. Mather is a more rustic site with few bathrooms and water spigots, and all were located quite a distance from each other.

Skies had been clear for several days and the temperature

had dropped to a comfortable 80-85 degrees and more good weather was predicted.

Steve was excited about camping again and energetically set up camp. He had a process now and wanted to do it all himself. He instructed me to find out where the store was so we could stock our cooler for a few days and locate firewood (you had to buy it, not collect down wood). The tent went up quickly, and by noon we were walking to the canyon rim to do some exploring.

It was mid-September. Family vacations were over. The visitors there now came with a deliberate, heart-pounding desire to see the Grand Canyon this time of year when most of the crowds had gone home to their jobs and obligations.

Those deliberate travelers included Europeans (I counted eight distinct accents), some honeymooners, and lots of singles, seniors, and serious hikers with sturdy boots and layered clothing. I guessed the boys from Moab had come to the GC, too. There were plenty of young, tanned, and handsome men with tight legs and broad shoulders, all carrying backpacks the size of a small person.

After hiking around the rim the first day, I knew I wanted to hike down one of the trails—at least part of the way. I thought I would have to bribe Steve with the promise of a T-shirt that read, "I Hiked the Grand Canyon", but I didn't. I bought the T-shirt anyway.

We reviewed the map and decided on the three-mile round-trip hike to the first rest stop on the Bright Angel Trail.

Although three miles is not a long hike, I knew that hiking in the Grand Canyon comes with an extreme set of challenges. But friendly backpackers were always on the watch for struggling tourists. If you stood around long enough looking confused and stupid, a couple of nice hikers would provide water and encouragement. And we did. At one point, I pulled to the side to rest on a rock and drink some water. Almost immediately, two twenty-something men stopped to inquire if we needed any help.

"We're fine, my mom's just tired."

Thanks, Steve, I said that to myself, but he was right. Going downhill was hard, and there was loose gravel and a lot of tight turns. His legs didn't seem to mind.

"Coming back up is going to take at least twice as long," they said. "And it will seem much steeper than going down, so take your time. You don't want to get rescued out of here. If you have a problem, we'll be coming back this way in about eight hours."

The next day I didn't feel tired—I felt energized, so we decided to take the trail again but leave early so it wouldn't be as hot. We ate a real breakfast, packed a variety of carb snacks, dried fruit, juice, and extra water, and headed down the crowded trail to the three-mile rest stop. It was easier going down that time. There were lots of people on the trail and all of them were friendly. People were stopped all along the trail, either resting or eating. They were usually the people on their way back up. Everyone talked to each other as they passed or asked if you needed assistance if you were sitting. There was communal energy—a bond of spirit and reverence for the Canyon and for those that make even the feeblest attempts to experience it. To Steve's delight, one man joined us and hiked along with us much of the way down.

We stopped and talked to two young men that were coming up the trail and had stopped to rest. We asked if they needed anything. They had enormous packs on their backs and told us they had been down all the way to the Colorado River, some twenty miles into the canyon. They had done this hike several times, they said, but this time was harder because of the heat. They thanked us for asking but said they were fine, so Steve and I continued down the trail and several hours later we got back to the top.

People pulling into the campsite next to us at 10 PM woke us up. We had gone to bed at 9 PM exhausted. I woke in the middle of the night with back pain from sleeping on the ground. The egg-crate mattress pad under the sleeping bag wasn't enough. I twisted and turned and tried to get comfortable and listened to the sounds outside the tent. I wanted to take aspirin, but that would have required a whole food-eating thing, getting up, finding water, so I lay there.

The wind whistled through the trees, but the tent never moved. Frogs and crickets hummed through the night. Occasional small footprint-sounds moved around just outside the tent, maybe a fox or a rabbit, but I didn't get up to look. Mostly, there was silence and stillness and an increasing dull ache in my back.

The ancients thought of this place as holy ground, but you don't need a religious experience to be inspired and humbled by the nature and energy of the Grand Canyon. Nothing can make you feel so small as to be at its mercy or experience the purity of it in a place as majestic as this.

Except...

The rim has been adulterated by us—people so eager to see it we've allowed buses and helicopters to assault the serenity and gift shops and restaurants to alter its shape and true purpose. No small footprints here. Thankfully, the greater whole of the Canyon has few or no human footprints at all, and that's what still makes it a place everyone should see.

Sitting on a small rise on the rim of the Grand Canyon, I faced the gaping hole in the earth and watched the sun set on the striations of rock just as it did a million years ago. Tears fell for no reason as I realized why it had been so necessary to do this trip. I wanted to see the world as it really was. I wanted to remember the magnificence, soak up the peacefulness that I lost somewhere between the meaningless marketing projects, endless bills, personal tragedies, and frustrations of marriage, not just those of my own, but others I knew. I thought I would find it in the eyes and hearts of most of the people I encountered, and it was there in some. It was absent in many.

I don't believe that most people are deliberately mean or difficult, even the Navajo women I encountered a few days ago. Most people are just afraid and defensive, ironically, defending themselves against the systems that used to inspire them.

Sometimes I want to run and hide in a place like this. Other times I want to help, stay in the big city, and make some personal contribution that attempts to change the world. Most of the time I am caught in the middle with everyone else—one foot stuck squarely in my material being.

But this journey of three months was almost over. We are nearly home and then it all begins again.

Road Noise

Vortex to Go

Sedona to Phoenix, Arizona

Steve slapped the hood of the car as he bolted past toward the red rock boulder cliffs. We had just wound around and up to the top of a cliff side in the Sedona hills near Cathedral Rock for a little hiking.

"You're not a bad driver, Mom. That was cool. Are you bringing lunch? Let's eat on the trail in thirty minutes."

Recently, Steve had become decisive about time. Some sort of organizational evolution. He wanted to do something in thirty minutes or forty. Specifics. Was it a new sign of adulthood—the attempt to master time? Soon, he would discover another sign of adulthood—time will not be mastered. We are at its mercy.

My back was reminding me of that as I dug around in my backpack. *Ahhh.* My fingers located the little plastic case at the far bottom. In a quick motion, I tossed a Fioricet onto my tongue and tipped the water bottle skyward. It wouldn't do much for my back, but I would care less.

"Meat! What are you doing? Are you bringing lunch?"

Steve's voice shattered all the silent molecules that rushed around those deep rocks with nowhere to go. There was no sound but the air in my ears. No wind. No birds still up this time of the morning. No cars or people. It was only us on this rocky colorful mountain with Steve standing on the top of a pile of boulders about fifteen yards away, calling for food and hustle.

"Yes. I'm coming. With food. Hey, don't go too far until I get up there. And hey! Snake potential!" I yelled back.

"I know. You always say that."

I threw some food items and water into the pack, put on the foam visor with the Arizona beige lizards on it, added some cheap sunglasses, and looked in the side window of the car to fluff up the sides of my hair before hoisting the pack over my shoulders and following Steve up the rocks.

When I got to the top, Steve was sitting on a rocky overlook staring out into Sedona below. It seemed like the whole of Sedona could be seen. He was quiet for several moments longer than I expected.

"Are you okay?"

He rolled his eyes. "Yeah, just waiting for you."

We hiked in mostly silence, which was out of character but seemed natural that morning. Even Steve didn't seem to want to break the silence except for the show and tell of various path-side wildlife—mostly lizards he tracked down and occasionally caught. When he caught them, he was gentle and protective, even providing words of encouragement to those that had lost tails in the struggle for life.

"That one is smiling. He's cute." I pointed to a nondescript brown one sunning on a rock.

"I don't think he wants to be called cute, Mom. He's special. That's a Great Earless Lizard. You can tell by the black stripes in front of his back legs. See?"

"But no ears? That can't be good."

"Actually, it is good. He hears by ground vibrations, mostly. And he has ears, just not external holes. These guys are easy to find because they like being out in the day's heat."

Earless lizards. Who knew? I wasn't surprised he recognized and knew about the Great Earless Lizard. He had been studying his *Audubon Field Guide to Reptiles and Amphibians* book since we bought it early in the trip.

Sedona is about an hour south of Flagstaff and it was, perhaps, the biggest surprise of the trip. I had expected a desert—Arizona flats, low scrub, saguaro cactus, an ocean of beige with a little artsy town plunked into the center. Instead, it was every shade of red, orange, purple, and green. A tequila sunrise with a sprawling art town in the middle. The same landscape from the Grand Canyon winds through Flagstaff and uncurls into this red rock canyon that still sits at a 4,500-foot elevation. Surrounded by sandstone rock and several national forests there is little beige anywhere—instead, lots of trees including mesquite, Arizona cypress, Ponderosa pines, and twisted junipers.

The area is thick with energy and attitude and an almost odd sense of peace. The locals will tell you it's the vortexes without explanation as to what exactly that means. Others will say it's the iron in the sandstone or afternoon monsoons that bring massive and energetic lightning strikes. And some will say it's the red rock—the elements of earth matter that connect us to it—that heighten the senses, fusing a complex interaction of energies. Steve and I love science, particularly the concepts of the quantum world, and there is a thought that energy creates matter—that energy is primary and form secondary.

I explained the local theories about the vortexes to Steve, who instantly understood and had his own theory.

"I think it does feel peaceful here. But I think it feels peaceful anywhere there are lots of trees. They give off oxygen you know, and extra oxygen can make you feel calm and energized at the same time."

Another Sedona peacefulness theory. Well, whatever it is, the elements that converge in Sedona are real.

It had been a long day—the Cathedral Rock hike, a trek around the airport vortex, and a jeep tour of the local geology. We were tired. I wanted a shower and dinner at a nearby restaurant I had spotted earlier. Steve wanted to watch television in the room and eat from the cooler. We did both. After my usual set of home-alone instructions to Steve and a request to recite my cell phone number for the fiftieth time, I walked to the Hideaway, a common-looking Italian restaurant but with an outdoor balcony overlooking a shallow creek and the fiery hills. I stared out at a watercolor sunset—a hundred shades of pink, gray, and blue and heard the tumbling of distant shallow water. My head had muted the sounds of the restaurant, the chatter of the patrons and street noise to a distant hum just as the hypnotic song of the cicada began a precision chorus. My mind wandered to the book I was reading—James Gleick's *Chaos,* and I wondered if they were the periodical cicadas—the ones that emerge as a community every thirteen years.

Looking around the restaurant I noticed, as usual, I was the only single person there. Everyone else was a couple or a family. It reminded me it was a Friday night, but that didn't bother me. Being alone never did. I ordered the penne, sipped my Dewar's neat, closed my eyes, and felt a sense of calm rush my head just as the scotch cooled my throat.

Back at the motel, Steve was in the same position as I had left him—still sitting on his bed watching television—but now surrounded by a sub-sandwich wrapper I had purchased earlier for him, an apple core, three empty juice boxes, a half-pint of chocolate milk and our last bag of dill pickle chips. I moved the trash and remaining pickle chips to my bed and scooted in beside him.

"Anything good on television? Did you miss me? Wanna play cards?"

"No, no, and yes. Crazy Eights."

"We're going to Slide Rock tomorrow. It's supposed to be cool—a natural rock water slide place. It's Saturday so maybe there will be some other kids there."

"Why do you worry about that? I don't need other kids around to have fun. You worry too much about me."

"You don't want me to worry about you?"

"No. Who's dealing?"

"What if I can't stop worrying about you—ever? I'll deal first."

"Then you'll live a wasted life. Go. Deal. Is Slide Rock far?"

Slide Rock was only a few miles north of Sedona in Oak Creek Canyon, and it is the ultimate water-slide park without the food vendors and street noise. Although the water was cool since it was previously ice, the shallow creek, flat rock, and sheltered canyon warm it up just enough.

Within an hour, Steve had delighted two college girls. It turned out they were from Los Gatos, our hometown, and lived only a couple of miles from us. One worked in a bakery we frequented. Serendipity. Again.

I laid back on the blanket-covered rock and put my foam Arizona lizard visor over my eyes. I might end up with a weird-looking sunburn, but I wasn't worried. That afternoon at Slide Rock, in the greater vortex of Sedona, I was not worried about anything. Maybe I didn't need to worry so much about Steve. He knew stuff—odd stuff, which meant he knew lots of other stuff, too. He made friends everywhere. He was cautious and seemed to have an inherent insight into people. He was a strong and healthy kid who was not afraid to speak up or stake a claim and say no. And I was beginning to think that maybe all my guilt and subsequent efforts to overcompensate for all the failings of the marriage to his father was working. He was the young man I was trying to shape. And better yet, he had escaped the influence of my dimmer sides—the tantrums, the seriousness, the hermit.

I watched from across the creek as the Los Gatos girls helped him out of the water, I knew he didn't need me. Not really. He would always have friends—and that was because he wasn't like me.

. . .

I looked over at Steve in the passenger seat. He was drawing something on a Post-it. He liked Post-its—paper his size that stuck to things. The best invention since the microwave oven. It was a cartoon flipbook. Probably his fifth on this trip. All the action sequences were drawn in the bottom left corner of the Post It. Of course. He was left-handed.

"What are you drawing?"

Without looking up he said, "An Earthworm Jim flipbook. Almost done, then I'll demonstrate. Do you know what a flipbook is? It's how they draw cartoons. Now, it's all on the computer, but it's still the same idea."

I examined his face. He still had a child's nose and skin, but his body was changing. He had gained a few preteen pounds— the slowed metabolism just before the teen growth spurt. He had always been strong, healthy, tall for his age, active, and busy. Always busy. Not irritable. Not a crybaby.

"We're almost to Phoenix. Then the next day we'll be in Southern California for a couple of days before we head home. Are you excited to get home?"

"Yeah, I want to see all my friends. And I need to go to school."

"I'm ready to go home, too. So, do you have some favorite parts of the trip?"

"The swamp, maybe. That aquarium with the white alligator. The horseback riding to the cave and I liked that beach where we stayed where the ocean was really warm."

"What about least favorites?"

"I didn't like it when you cried and got all mad because it was raining. That was dumb. You can't do anything about the weather, you know. You get mad about dumb stuff. And you worry all the time."

Right. He didn't miss anything.

Acts of Redemption

Southern California to Home

Four hours of driving disappeared into the night. Before I knew it, the dark early hours on Highway 10 out of Phoenix opened up a bright, warm morning as I pulled into a gas station in Blythe. Blythe was one of many of the most unremarkable towns I had been through in all my years of driving around California. That late-September morning was no better and no worse. It was a blank slate so dull no color came to mind.

The short-term memory of a dirty gray gas stop where I handed a tall twenty-something man $30 in cash slapping it twice on the counter and saying 'thirty on two' faded to a thud when I pulled out of the station.

It would be a couple more hours before hitting the eastern outskirts of Greater Los Angeles, flying through Coachella and Indio like a Santa Ana wind to spend a few days visiting friends in Southern California before the drive home to Los Gatos.

We spent the week recalling tales of the trip. What were our favorite places? Did we get to Ouray? What interesting travelers did we meet? I recalled standing on a ridge above the

Snake River just outside Jackson Hole, taking pictures of the wildflowers and visualizing scenes from the old West, hiking rocky red Moab, and breathing in the damp forests of the Adirondacks. My favorite things were the backroads and quiet moments standing at the edge of an ocean, shallow waves rolling over my toes. And it surprised me at the ease of engaging in meaningful conversation with strangers in over thirty states that often led to a revelation of our shared concerns and passions.

Day eighty-seven of the trip was September 20. We were in Palm Springs and two days away from home. An earthquake in the Ridgecrest sequence shook us out of bed that morning. I bolted straight up like a startled cat but had to awaken Steve to go sit in the hallway.

It was a fitting end, a jolt back to reality. What was this odyssey? Did it change anything? Did I feel different that morning? What epiphany was I expecting? A vision? A voice in my head offering a magic solution to problems I hadn't fully identified? Did I recognize a profound personality change while driving around the US for 90 days? If so, it was subtle or would be recognizable only after the dust settled and the car engine cooled.

That morning, only a few things were clear. Reality was swiftly coming into focus. I was concerned about finding a job quickly. I also knew I would be far more selective in my relationships with men and that there was a possibility I would never again be in a long-term relationship, and I had made peace with that. I swore I would rely on my intuition more and not constantly second guess myself. I would say *no* more often to the adults in my life and *yes* more often to my son.

I was already regretting some things. I took it hard when things didn't go smoothly and held on too tightly to things that didn't matter and with that, missed the underlying lesson. I knew I didn't want to make that mistake again, yet it seemed like a fundamental personality problem that wouldn't easily be eliminated.

But what about Steve? What impression did he have from this three-month ramble through the US? Was he worse or better for it? Was he tougher, stronger, smarter? A few years from now will he forget my weaknesses, or remember that I ranted about weather, misplaced road signs, and dirty motel rooms? Will he remember that we also laughed a lot? Will he remember he made people laugh and that many will probably remember him—that clever young man they met on their vacation?

On Saturday, September 23, day ninety of the trip, we were on the way home to Los Gatos. Rising up through the Grapevine and the long shadows of the sunrise, we reached the yellow-gold silence of a long stretch of Interstate 5 farmland. Its familiarity was comforting—a variety of vegetables, fruit, nut, and olive trees blooming, dust spiraling behind a tractor, the arms of a center pivot spraying water into a field—a slice of the cycle of cultivated human existence.

I had driven that route up the middle of California many

times. I had all the markers memorized, ticking off the miles ahead. Buttonwillow, Harris Ranch, where the cows waited, oblivious to be processed, Pacheco Pass, once a stagecoach and mail route connecting travelers to San Francisco, Gilroy, and its overwhelming smell of garlic certain times of the year, and then we were almost home. At that moment, all the problems that hung dark over me flattened out over acres of green simplicity and seemed like just another page in a boring novel. But if you try to hold the thought of that simplicity and find contentment, it leaks from your fingers like melting ice.

If I were to map out the history of my life to date, I wonder if it would be as it seems. Like this landscape, life has distinct cycles of rest and growth—good times and bad that roll in like waves and recede again, allowing us time to assess our lives and the inevitable change we call time. True change cannot be completed in a few months, but it takes years to recover from a loss or to move from ecstasy to simple comfort and back again. Forever, the pendulum swings, only briefly passing through those times of pure contentment before making another full extension to some new pain or pleasure requiring both acts of redemption and shouts of joy.

Epilogue

Although I started writing this book in 1997, it was mostly just converting my paper journals to digital. It took many years to find the time and make some sense of the notes and thoughts I sketched out during the trip.

Here's what happened when I got home.

As soon as I got home from the journey, I was distracted back into my normal life. At first, I didn't notice the change, but my life took an important turn for the better immediately. Serendipity? I've used that term several times in this book and never gave it much thought before the trip.

A month prior to the trip, I put an ad in the local Los Gatos paper for a three-month sublet of my apartment. One man answered the ad. Not only was he the only one that answered, but he was also the perfect person to answer my ad. He also paid me for the whole three months in advance because he didn't want me to change my mind and come home early!

Two days after getting back, I had a long conversation with him. He was a management consultant for a Cambridge UK company starting up an American operation that was literally two miles from my home. Within two weeks, I met with the president who hired me to do a marketing analysis report and within the month I was offered a job as the vice president of marketing for the advanced technology company. Within two months, I was in London meeting the team.

Was that just an accident? Just a coincidence? I don't think it was, but I was so distracted with getting back to my life of details, I didn't notice the significance of those converging forces. My life seemed to be continuing as before; Steve was back in school, I was working, doing laundry, paying bills, and driving Steve and his friends to the arcades every weekend. I was also falling into bed at 10 PM exhausted, just like always. Yet everything had changed.

I can sum up the change in a few brief words: Acute observation, a broader perspective, and increased confidence. Those words seem simple, but they are the overarching reasons my life got better after the journey. I assume those abilities were always within me, I just wasn't using them. I hadn't recognized them, or they had gotten lost along the way.

After the journey, my perspective shifted dramatically as well as my way of observing what was happening around me. For years, maybe most of my life, I paid attention to the wrong things. I was bent on *improving* myself instead of *being* myself. I was trying to improve my life without observing who I was. I think we all need to improve ourselves, but maybe the reasoning behind that is just an illusion because we all think we're less than we are. Instead of focusing on improving, we need to focus on discovering. What I needed was to pay attention to the things that didn't seem significant. The journey kept showing me those things. It kept pointing out things that I otherwise would have missed.

I am convinced it was because I took the time, removed myself from the external distractions and voices of friends, family, work, and relationships that allowed me the space to observe what was going on around me and around my son. The journey forced me to pay attention to the little things that didn't seem significant before and pushed me into a higher level of confidence so I could truly see who I was and what I was capable of doing.

Road Noise

Acknowledgments

Thank you to those we met along the way that showed kindness to two strangers without judgment, odd looks, and overcharges. This includes the owners of the Marsh Plains Motel in Vermont, the traveling gospel singers we met in Panama City Beach, the manager of the Crockett Hotel in San Antonio, and every single one of the travelers we met at hostels who offered food, words of encouragement, and intriguing adventure stories. Thanks to all those we met on trails who were so quick to offer support. Thanks to those in southern New Mexico who waved to strangers for no reason at all.

Thanks to Steve's teacher and the Principal of Fisher Middle School for so quickly welcoming this *virtual classroom* project, something unheard of at the time.

And most of all, thanks to Steve my traveling companion who, as a child and as an adult, has always allowed me the freedom to be who I am, forgiving my inadequacies as a mother and applauding my need to explore. Thank you for enduring the divorce of your parents and somehow rising above it all.

Road Noise